Taxation Planning for
Middle East Operations

Taxation Planning for Middle East Operations

A Research Study sponsored by the Kuwait Office of Peat, Marwick, Mitchell & Co. and presented for the obtainment of the final degree of Ecole Supérieure des Sciences Fiscales, Brussels

by

ROSE M.CLERIN-LISON

1978

Springer-Science+Business Media, B.V.

Cover design: Pieter J. van der Sman

ISBN 978-90-200-0515-8 ISBN 978-94-017-4477-5 (eBook)

DOI 10.1007/978-94-017-4477-5

Originally published by KLuwer, Deventer, The Netherlands in 1978.

Preface

If investment in the EEC countries has been the major preoccupation of the international business community in the 1960's, contracting in the Arab states seems to become one of the major trends of the 1970's. The need for multicountry business and tax information was felt simultaneously. Language difficulties, scarcity of legal and other sources, distance and, most of all, the novelty of business expansion in this direction made such information still more necessary than in the European or inter-American setting.

A few symposiums were held, corporate and tax laws were translated, research studies were initiated, among which the book of Mr and Mrs SHILLING on Doing Business in Saudi Arabia and the Arab Gulf States, a rich mine of general business information. I was therefore very pleased when Mrs CLERIN, completing her tax studies at Ecole Supérieure des Sciences Fiscales in Brussels, mentioned that she was going to live in the Middle East, had the opportunity to work with a well-known international accounting firm and proposed to focus her final dissertation at the School on the tax planning of operations in Arab countries. She devoted months of research to the study of sources both in Middle East and in industrialized Western countries, to come up with a true planning study, clear, readable and practical. The description of the tax and corporate structure of the operating territories will be found in the first half of the book. The treatment of income in the investor's country is described in the final part of the work. Planning considerations are present through the book and will stimulate the exercise of tax and business judgment in structuring operations. It may also remind legislators and treaty negotiators of lost opportunities. As Mrs CLERIN rightly puts it, where tax exemptions are granted in the Middle East on the condition that the tax benefit is not lost locally, an intermediate company may have to be used. As early as 1957, Mr Dan T. SMITH, Deputy to the Secretary of the Treasury, testified before the US Senate Foreign Relations Committee in saying that 'operation of the present law in effect nullifies the tax concessions that foreign countries make' and that 'the tax sparing laws should be recognized subject to appropriate safeguards'. The Middle East is a vast field not only for industrial and business development, but also for improved legislation and cooperative treaty making.

Jacques MALHERBE
Avocat, Brussels bar
Professor of International Tax Law
at Ecole Supérieure des Sciences Fiscales

Contents

Introduction

Businessmen, Contractors, Bankers, Traders doing business in the Middle East are often surprised to learn that they could become liable to tax in most of the States.

In their rush for contracts, many tend to neglect to ascertain the tax legislation in force relying on a general belief that all these States are tax havens and that contracts are tax exempt. The reality is very different since most of the Middle East States have tax decrees. Only a few States have no tax law and even in these no guarantee exists that this situation will continue. Some States already enforce the tax legislation whilst others have hitherto mainly taxed oil companies. If the situation sounds like paradise today, the signs are there to indicate that this will not last.

— Government officials have stated the need to enforce taxes to increase consciousness of National Identity,
— In Kuwait, one of the very richest in per capita terms, foreign corporate entities trading in the State have recently been asked to fill in tax returns.

It is however true that many of the Gulf States do have sufficient monetary reserves not to be concerned with taxing foreign interests and to use tax exemptions for their citizens as a business incentive or a way of redistributing the oil income.

This publication has been aimed at making investors conscious that tax problems may arise, and that the tax position of potential contracts in the Middle East should be analysed as carefully as they would be if the activity were to be contemplated in any industrialised country; it also considers the practical problems that tend to face the foreign company seeking to operate in the Middle East State either as a manufacturing investor or as a contractor.

The framework is to consider:

— Structure and Planning for operations in Middle East States,
— The system of taxation of foreign capital in force in selected Middle East operating territories,
— The system of taxing foreign income in force in 'key' investors States.

It should be emphasized that the publication is concerned with general principles and cannot therefore be regarded as providing specific guidance for particular cases; it does however seek to draw attention to the strategies that are available and the type of situation in which they are likely to be most appropriate.

The detailed information set out in this publication is based on the legislation and official practice in force on 30th of June 1977.

The geographic coverage has been limited to:
— Key investing or supplier States to the Middle East,
— Key Middle East States,
— Selected locations for intermediate and tax haven companies.

The choice within each category has inevitably been somewhat arbitrary and a case can be clearly made for including other States. The States considered are:

Investor	*Middle East*	*Haven*
Belgium	Egypt	Ajman
France	Iraq	Bahrain
Germany	Saudi Arabia	Bermuda
Japan	Sudan	Netherlands
Netherlands	*Gulf States*	Liberia
United Kingdom	Ajman*	Panama
United States	Abu Dhabi*	Ras Al-Khaimah
	Bahrain	
	Dubai*	
	Fujeirah*	
	Kuwait	
	Oman	
	Qatar	
	Ras Al-Khaimah*	
	Sharjah*	
	Umm Al-Qawain*	

* Member of the United Arab Emirates.

In considering any specific business decision, it must however, be strongly emphasized that many of the jurisdictions concerned interpret the legislation with a wide degree of administrative discretion, and it will often be desirable to review the facts of a particular case with the officials concerned prior to entering into a commitment.

In researching this book I have been much assisted by the Partners and tax staff of Peat, Marwick, Mitchell & Co. (and their associated firms) in the locations I have considered; my thanks are due to all of them.

Kuwait, September 1977 — Rose M. Clerin

Part I
Structure and Planning

Chapter I
Structure

Foreign investment is welcomed in the Arab States inasmuch as it assists in development and introduces latest technology. Keeping this in mind, it is most important that the foreign company is well informed about a number of key questions such as:

— Foreign exchange regulations,
— Prohibited activities,
— Employment of foreign nationals,
— Availability of labour.

Having knowledge of the requirements, and having analysed them in the light of particular circumstances, *it is then necessary to determine the manner in which the business is to be structured.* The key structural issues that require to be answered are:

— 'What types of corporate vehicle are available, and which should be adopted?';
— 'How should the investor's participation in the chosen vehicle be held?'.

Foreign investors are required to comply with the local company law and the basic law. The law is usually published by decree and amplified by subsequent administrative regulations.

Most Middle East countries have income tax laws, commercial and company law. A certain similarity exists between all of them, but it would certainly be a mistake to believe that the laws are the same everywhere and to think that what applies to one country applies necessarily to another country. It is therefore most important for any investor to appreciate:

— commercial law and the registration procedures can be very complex and detailed and should be analysed carefully — it is a misconception to believe that the Middle East is an easy area to do business in because the laws are still at an embryo stage or non-existent;
— general tax laws exist everywhere (except Bahrain and Fujeirah) — some countries enforce them, others are planning to do so in the future.

No attempt has been made in this publication to analyse in detail the differences between the laws of the different States; consideration is however given to the basic *structures* available to foreign investors doing business in the Middle East. Four basic types of structures are usually available.

Agency

In an agency situation, the foreign company merely sells to a local agent who is then solely responsible for all aspects. The agent himself employs any experts who may require to be stationed in the country.

Defining the extent of taxable income in the case of an agency involves in most States consideration of the classic distinction between 'trading in' and 'trading with'. Normally pure supply contracts are not taxable, but a contract including any activity in the customer state may be subject to taxation.

Sponsored Subcontractor

The foreign partner undertakes to carry out services on an agreed pricing basis as subcontractor to the local agent. In this case the foreign company trades in the Middle East under the form of a branch and in most cases branches are considered to be companies for tax purposes.

Joint Venture Branch

In a joint venture a contractual agreement is drawn up with the joint venturer who must be a National in most countries and will act also as sponsor. Profits, losses and finance are shared in the proportions agreed by the venturers. The foreign interest in the venture must usually be registered and may be subject to local tax.

Participation in a Legal Entity

In this case a legal entity is formed and this is the vehicle through which the parties' interests are channelled. Broadly, the choise will lie between two major types of corporate entity:

— limited liability partnerships (often referred to as 'companies'),
— joint stock companies.

Here again most countries have a company law, but there might be substantial differences between them (capital requirements, number of partners, amount of capital to be paid up at the formation of the company).

For example: In Kuwait a 'With Limited Liability Partnership' ('WLL') is an association of natural persons; in Saudi Arabia, corporate persons may be members of a 'Limited Liability Partnership' ('LLP'). In Kuwait a 'WLL' can never have more than 30 partners; in Saudi Arabia a 'LLP' may include 50 partners.

Depending on the personal needs of the investor, there may be important reasons for choosing one particular entity instead of another. Each case here is unique and should be analysed carefully. Pertinent factors to be considered are as follows:
— Degree of control,
— Transfer of shares (option to disengage),
— Taxation,
— Activity restrictions,
— Capital contributions.

Degree of Control

Where the foreign investor is required to be a minority shareholder, operating control can be achieved by entering into a management contract with the majority shareholder. In such cases, day-to-day management functions are delegated to the foreign company through appointed foreign directors. As compensation for its management services, the foreign national may take a fee and/or share in the profits, but this will be the subject of negotiations between the parties.

Transfer of Shares

A key factor in the structuring of operations abroad is the maintenance of the investor's option to disengage. The law usually contains provisions on the negotiability of shares depending on the structure adopted. The company's statutes may however extend such provisions and further define the negotiability of the shares.

Taxation

Depending on the structure adopted, tax rates might vary (e.g. Iraq, Sudan); tax liability may also vary according to the structure chosen. For example in a country where the individual is not taxed, the creation of a 'WLL' may result in tax not being assessed in practice, as it is by definition an association of natural persons.

Activity Restrictions

Apart from the fact that foreign nationals in many Gulf States are excluded from engaging in certain activities (banking, real estate) the structure to be adopted by the foreign investor might depend on the type of activity involved. Generally speaking not all types of corporate entities are available for all kinds of activities. Limited Liability Partnerships for example may usually not engage in insurance, commercial banking or investment banking. Such is the case in Kuwait and Saudi Arabia.

Capital Contributions

An important factor to take into consideration is the minimum capital requirements which vary substantially from State to State. (See table following page).

MINIMUM CAPITAL REQUIREMENTS FOR COMPANIES**

State	Partnership		Joint stock company		Remarks
	Local Currency	Amount in US $ 000's	Local Currency	Amount in US $ 000's	
Ajman*	—	—	—	—	No minimum capital requirements
Abu Dhabi	—	—	DH 300,000	77	
Bahrain	BD 10,000	25	BD 200,000	505	Private Company
			BD 500,000	1,265	Public Company
Dubai*	—	—	—	—	No minimum capital requirements
Fujeirah	—	—	—	—	No minimum capital requirements
Kuwait	KD 7,500	26	KD 7,500	26	Private Company
			KD 37,000	131	Public Company
Oman	OR 10,000	29	OR 25,000	72	OR 150,000 if foreign interests included in Joint Stock Company.
Qatar	—	—	QR 100,000	25	Private Company
			QR 500,000	126	Public Company
Ras Al-Khaimah*	—	—	—	—	No minimum capital requirements
Saudi Arabia	SR 50,000	14	SR 200,000	57	Private Company
			SR 1,000,000	283	Public Company
Sharjah*	—	—	—	—	No minimum capital requirements
Umm Al-Qawain*	—	—	—	—	No minimum capital requirements

* In these Emirates there is no commercial or company law and no distinction is made between joint stock companies and limited liability partnerships.

** The local currencies and their US dollar equivalents as of June 30, 1977, are listed on page 52.

Notes

— Foreign companies are generally not allowed to participate in the capital of public companies in Kuwait.

— Paid in capital in joint stock companies upon subscription must be at least 20 or 25%. The balance should be fully paid after 4 or 5 years. In Saudi Arabia paid in capital upon subscription should be at least 50%, but the law does not draw a time limit to have the capital fully paid. In Abu Dhabi all shares must be fully paid up on subscription.

— In the case of Limited Liability partnerships in Bahrain, Kuwait, Oman Qatar, Saudi Arabia the capital should be fully paid upon subscription.

— Legal reserves of 10% of the net annual profits are usually required except in the States where no company law has been enacted.

— Iraq has not been included in the list since foreign companies usually create branches instead of legal entities.

Chapter II
Other Factors

Companies deciding to do business in the Middle East should adopt a flexible attitude and in some cases several structures in the life of a project can be very beneficial. Special forms of contracts may at times be negotiated for example contracts with tax reimbursement provisions. Also the Middle East being an area of tremendous expansion a great deal of the business takes the form of a single business contract, a few words should be said about contractors in general. There is discussed below:
— Change of a branch into a subsidiary
— Contracts with tax reimbursement provisions
-- Contractors generally

Change of a Branch into a Subsidiary

In many large projects it is not likely that a single business form is a suitable vehicle for the whole of the cycle of operations intended. Very often from a fiscal point of view, it is appropriate that a branch structure be adopted in the early stages if losses are being incurred as these may be available for relief against Head Office profits.

When operations become profitable, a corporate entity might be created to replace the branch. In such cases, care should be taken to ascertain the exact situation in the investors' own country. Some countries have set up rules for the recapture of the prior years' losses and in other countries the tax authorities will want to be satisfied that the commercial justification for the transaction outweighs any loss of tax revenue.

The change of a branch into a subsidiary can for example be considered for investments in Egypt where starting business with a branch would be helpful from a practical point of view in that the formalities for establishing a branch are rather simpler than those required to establish a company. The branch could later on be transformed to an exempt company (Free Zone company or non-Free Zone Company), and in this way full advantage can be taken of the tax exemption period.

Contracts with Tax Reimbursement Provisions

In Saudi Arabia the great majority of contracts are taxable, but in a few cases, reimbursement is granted. Before 1971 government sponsored exempt contracts were common, but since then total exemption is no longer possible. The key paragraph of the decree states that government contracts concluded with foreign companies or contractors can no longer be concluded on a tax exempt basis, 'but it is possible, if it is found in the public interest, to include a provision obliging the contractor to pay all the taxes on the specified dates and then ask the administrative department with which the contract is concluded to reimburse him, in the light of the evidence and documents proving the payment of such taxes to the Zakat and Income tax Department'.

In cases where it is possible, such a structure is clearly advantageous, but each situation does of course require a detailed analysis to ascertain the domestic tax position. It is considered however that if the contractual documents establish the reimbursement as a contract price adjustment, the case for stating that the profits have been subject to tax abroad and therefore eligible for relief becomes stronger.

Contractors Generally

Given the pace of infrastructure development in the Middle East, much foreign commercial activity is of a 'one-off contract' nature and in this situation the foreign contractor will normally wish to adopt the simplest structure possible.

This is traditionally the branch of the contractor or a company controlled by the contractor.

Two basic questions are:

- Can the branch be wholly foreign controlled?
- Is a National sponsor needed and if so are special conditions attached to his employment?

State	Is wholly foreign control permissible?	Is a National Sponsor needed?	Notes
Ajman	yes	no	
Abu Dhabi	yes	yes	1
Bahrain	no	yes	2
Dubai	yes	no	3
Egypt	yes	no	
Fujeirah	yes	no	
Iraq	yes	no	
Kuwait	no	yes	4
Oman	yes	no	5
Qatar	yes	yes	6
Ras Al-Khaimah	yes	no	3
Saudi Arabia	yes	yes	7
Sharjah	yes	no	3
Sudan	yes	no	
Umm Al-Qawain	yes	no	

Notes

1. Abu Dhabi: National sponsor is required by all contractors and his remuneration is limited in respect of Public Sector contracts by a sliding scale ranging from 1% to 2% dependent on the size of the contract.

2. Bahrain: Any foreign business activity (other than a branch which must have a sponsor) must cede at least 51% of the profits to Bahraini interests, although contractual arrangements can effectively override this.

3. Dubai, Sharjah, Ras Al-Khaimah: Companies wishing to obtain a licence in the absence of a sponsor will be asked to deposit a bond of DH 100,000 as guarantee.

4. Kuwait: Any foreign business activity must cede at least 51% of the profits to Kuwaiti interests, although contractual arrangements can effectively override this.

5. Oman: Only Nationals or Nationally controlled companies can act as Commercial Agents.

6. Qatar: As an exception to the provisions requiring that only Qatari individuals and companies may be practising the business of contracts of works in Qatar, non-Qatari individuals and companies may be allowed to execute contracting work by a Decree in accordance with a proposal by the Deputy Ruler provided that the purpose of this exception is to facilitate a public service or to realise a public benefit.

No foreign contracting company shall have permission to practice business in Qatar, unless it appoints a service agent whose nationality is Qatari. The functions of the service agent shall be confined to facilitating relations between the company and the authorities.

7. Saudi Arabia: In some cases government agencies themselves act as the sponsor to foreign contractors.

Chapter III
Branch or Company

In contrast to contracting activity which tends to take branch form (by reason of its transient nature) foreign investors participating in service or manufacturing activity will need to consider whether they should seek to incorporate a Nationally registered entity and if so, the extent to which National capital should be invited to participate.

The key question is whether foreign interests can control Nationally incorporated entities and if so, on what condition.

The table and notes below summarise the position in very general terms:

State	Can foreign interests control Nationally incorporated entities?	Notes
Ajman	yes	
Abu Dhabi	no	1
Bahrain	no	2
Dubai	yes	
Egypt	yes	3
Fujeirah	yes	
Iraq	no	4
Kuwait	no	5
Oman	yes	6
Qatar	no	7
Ras Al-Khaimah	yes	
Saudi Arabia	yes	8
Sharjah	yes	
Sudan	yes	9
Umm Al-Qawain	yes	

Notes

1. Abu Dhabi: At least 51% of National participation will be required.

2. Bahrain: National interests are normally required to have 51% control.

3. Egypt: Wholly foreign control is permissable in the Free Zone projects (Law 43 Free Zone Company).

In the non-Free Zone projects in practice Egyptian participation should be at least 25% (Law 43 non-Free Zone Company).

4. Iraq: National (or in some circumstances Arab) capital must have at least 51% control.

5. Kuwait: National capital must have at least 51% control. Public Joint Stock Companies must be 100% controlled by National interests.

6. Oman: In the case of normal commercial companies, National interests must have at least a 35% interest; the exceptions are that development projects or specifically exempted companies can have a 100% foreign interest and certain types of activity require a higher Omani interest than 35%, these are:

— Press and Publicity	66%
— Public Utility	51%
— Real Estate	51%
— Shipping or Aircraft	51%

7. Qatar: National capital must have at least 51% control.

8. Saudi Arabia: Public Joint Stock Companies are normally controlled by National interests; in order to qualify for five year tax holidays, companies set up to carry out development projects must have at least 25% National capital.

9. Sudan: Each new entity requires Government approval and in practice National control is normally retained.

Chapter IV
Taxation of Commercial Income

The basic considerations here are:
- the type of taxation system in force,
- the availability of incentive legislation.

Each is discussed below:

The Systems

The tax position of the different States can be divided into three main categories:
- The States which levy taxes on corporate foreign entities or foreign branches (Egypt, Iraq, Oman, Saudi Arabia, Sudan);
- The States which have issued tax decrees of general application, but where it has not been the historic practice of the Taxation Authorities to make assessments on companies other than oil companies (Abu Dhabi, Dubai, Kuwait[1], Qatar, Sharjah);
- The States where tax decrees have either not been issued or not utilised (Ajman[2], Bahrain[3], Fujeirah[4], Ras Al-Khaimah[2], Umm Al-Qawain[2]).

Foreign companies doing business in the Middle East should be very careful if they decide to implement their operations in a State which does not at present have any taxation system or where the tax decrees are not enacted. At any time a decision might change this situation, and if the facility is available, use should be made of the incentive legislation which many States provide for development projects. In these cases National participation is almost always a requirement and tax exemptions vary between 5 and 10 years depending on the State concerned.

Incentive Legislation

A number of Arab States have legislation providing for substantial tax

1. But see page 82.
2. Ajman, Ras Al-Khaimah and Umm Al-Qawain have not utilised their tax decrees.
3. The tax decree in Bahrain only deals with oil companies.
4. Fujeirah has not issued a tax decree of general application.

incentives available to foreign investors who meet the particular qualifications set out in the law concerned.

ABU DHABI[5]

Any industrial company which satisfies certain conditions, can be granted exemption from income tax on profits for the first five years of operation, and from income tax on reserve funds set aside from the projects after the five-year period, if these reserve funds are used for improvement or expansion purposes and provided that they do not amount to more than 50% of the total annual profits.

Sites may also be assigned to a company free of rent for five years.

In any case, Abu Dhabian participation in the capital of the project must not be less than 51%.

DUBAI

There is currently no incentive legislation in Dubai, but it is understood that exemptions can be granted by Amiri Decree.

EGYPT[6]

Approved development projects in the Free Zones are exempted indefinitely from corporate income tax. Tax exemption is also granted for a period from 5 to 8 years to companies engaged on investment projects outside the Free Zones in respect of undistributed profits.

IRAQ[7]

Legislation was designed to facilitate duly registered foreign branches engaged in work relating to major development projects. Fiscal exemption is granted to approved projects, but no exchange control exemptions are available nor are there any personal taxation benefits for the employees engaged on the project (both foreign and local).

5. Abu Dhabi Law of Industry 1967.
6. Egypt Law 43 for 1974.
7. Iraq Law 157 for 1973.

KUWAIT[8]

If the project is of an 'industrial' nature, which would normally mean that the Kuwait operation must contain a significant added value, the Industrial Law provides for tax holidays of up to 10 years in cases approved by the Ministry of Commerce and Industry.

There is however no exemption available from the agency or Kuwaiti participation laws which require 51% Kuwaiti participation in companies formed under Kuwaiti law or branches registered as doing business in Kuwait.

OMAN

Companies whose principal activity is industrial, agricultural or fishing are exempted for five years from the date of their establishment, companies with a paid up capital of more than OR 100,000 and which contribute to the progress of National Economic Development within the Sultanate may be exempted for a period of five years by the Minister of Commerce and Industry. This period can be extended for a further five years.

QATAR[9]

The profits of Qatari 'share' companies whose purpose is to establish and operate a project necessary for the support and development of the national economy (whether in the field of industry, agriculture, commerce, mining, construction of viaducts or bridges or means of communication or hotels or the reclamation of waste land) may be exempted for a period of 5 years from income tax.

As in Kuwait there is no exemption available from Qatari participation laws which require 51% Qatari participation in shareholding companies.

SAUDI ARABIA[10]

The incentives available are subject to a minimum Saudi participation of 25% and approval of the project by the Ministry of Industry & Electricity. A tax holiday of five years can be granted to investors in 'economic development projects'.

The term 'economic development project' has been widely interpreted

8. Kuwait Industrie Act.
9. Decree Law 3 for 1966 (Amendment of Income Tax Decree).
10. Saudi Arabia (Law 35 of 1383)

by the Ministry, particularly in cases where the Saudi interest has been 50% or more, and it would appear that a number of foreign concerns primarily operating as contractors have been granted this status on condition that the Saudi interest was 50%, particularly where the project includes a significant 'manufacturing' element.

SHARJAH

There is currently no incentive legislation in Sharjah.

SUDAN[11]

Concessions include corporate tax exemptions for up to five years and industrial land at concessionary prices.

AJMAN, BAHRAIN, FUJEIRAH, RAS AL-KHAIMAH, UMM AL-QAWAIN

There is currently no incentive legislation in these States.

Conclusion

In order to obtain full benefit from such legislation, it is essential to examine the legislation of the investor's home country and at the same time consider whether the formation of an intermediate company (to hold the equity in the entity benefitting from the incentive) is desirable to reduce the overall taxation cost on the profits generated by the investment; some general considerations are set out below.

— For some of the investors' countries the tax holiday granted as development incentive will only result in domestic tax deferral (United States, Japan, United Kingdom).

— For some others (Belgium, Holland) the tax holiday granted in the investing country will not be lost because the law takes the view that since the foreign income has followed the tax regime applicable abroad, it is no longer subject to domestic taxes.

— The United Kingdom provides in some of its recent bilateral treaties with developing countries a tax sparing provision if the tax holiday is granted as a development incentive (e.g. Sudan, but this treaty has not yet been ratified).

— If certain conditions are met, dividends from a developing country are exempt in Germany.

11. Sudan, The Development Promotion of Industrial Investment Act 1972 and the Organisation and promotion of Investment in Economic Service Act of 1972.

Chapter V
Taxation Interactions

In deciding how to assemble a structure that is appropriate for particular circumstances, two factors are of great importance:

— the need to analyse the *total* impact of each alternative on the parties concerned;
— the importance that commercial considerations should be given in designing structure; once this has been determined, it is the function of the tax planner to optimise the fiscal position rather than to seek to dictate the structure itself.

The basic alternative strategies open to the planner normally depend on four variables:

— Is the income earned in the operating State taxable or exempt there?
— Is the foreign investor free to choose between the use of a branch or a subsidiary?
— Are losses in the early years of operation a probability?
— Will any purpose be served by the use of an intermediary company?

These issues are analysed below.

A. Where Branch Income Is Exempted Abroad

United Kingdom, United States, Germany, Belgium

— The branch income exempted in the foreign country will be subject at home to corporate tax without any relief.
— No withholding tax on the foreign income received will be levied.
— Losses of the foreign branch can be set off against other UK, US, German or Belgian taxable profit.
— If the exemption is the result of incentive legislation, the UK investor doing business in Sudan will be able to make use (once the bilateral treaty is ratified) of Article 23 (2) of the treaty, which provides that the foreign tax 'spared' under local incentive arrangements can be taken into account in computing UK double tax credit.[1]

1. See United Kingdom pages 133-134.

— The German investor under the Developing Countries Tax Law[2] will be able to provide for a tax deductible reserve of 100% or 40% of the investment. Amounts deducted must however be carried forward and minimum instalments (a sixth or a twelfth part depending on the nature of the investment) must be added to the taxable profits starting with the sixth year of the investment.

NETHERLANDS

— Income exempt abroad, but subject *in principle* to taxation, is exempted from corporate taxes at home.
— The branch moreover is not subject to any withholding tax on the foreign income received.
— Foreign losses can be deducted from Dutch taxable income.

FRANCE

— *The foreign branch profits* under the territoriality concept are segregated from French source income and are not liable to French taxation on income.
— Under certain circumstances, deductions can be made for losses and investment expenses[3], but such deductions must be recaptured,
— There is no withholding tax on the foreign income received.
— In the subsequent distribution of dividends, a *précompte* will be assessed, because the dividends result from profits which have not borne company tax in France.

B. Where the Income of a Subsidiary Is Exempted Abroad

UNITED STATES, UNITED KINGDOM

— The foreign dividends received will be liable to domestic corporate taxes.
— In the UK, exchange control rules may require remittance of 66% of the profits available for distribution.
— In the US, if the subsidiary is defined as a FPHC[4] undistributed income will be subject to tax as well. Otherwise a foreign subsidiary will make it possible to defer US tax on dividends.
— Foreign losses cannot be deducted from other taxable income.

2. See Germany pages 114-115.
3. See France page 105.
4. See United States page 140.

Germany

- — The provisions of the Developing Countries Tax Law will be applicable.
- — Undistributed profits can be subject to tax under the Aussensteuergesetz if they are taxed at a nil rate or at a rate of less than 30%.
- — Dividends from a developing country are exempt in Germany if the affiliation privilege is applicable.

Belgium

- — Foreign dividends qualifying as permanent investments[5] will benefit from the dividend income deduction and as a result in practice escape domestic corporate taxation.
- — There are no distribution requirements,
- — If losses occur in the foreign subsidiary, these will not be deductible from Belgian taxable income.

Netherlands

Foreign affiliates in which the Dutch company has a holding of at least 5% are not subject to Dutch taxation on dividends provided the Dutch authorities accept that:

- — the affiliation privilege[6] was applicable, because the Dutch company played an active commercial role;
- — foreign tax (whether levied or not) was applicable in principle and was a qualifying tax on income;
- — however, where no general tax decrees have been issued, i.e. Bahrain, Fujeirah, dividends from a qualifying investment will not be granted the corporate tax exemption in the Netherlands;
- — there are no distribution requirements at present, profits could therefore remain abroad and be used to finance other investments;
- — foreign losses cannot be deducted from Dutch income.

France

- — Articles 145 and 146 CGI[7] are of application and therefore dividends (in the case of 10% participation or shares of 10 million FF in another

5. See Belgium page 99.
6. See Netherlands page 124.
7. See France page 105.

entity) will not be included in the taxable base (except for 5% share of expenses).

- Under certain circumstances, deductions can be made for losses and investment expenses but such deductions must be recaptured.[8]
- In the subsequent distribution of dividends, a précompte will be assessed because the dividends result from profits which have not borne company tax in France.

C. Summary for Exempt Income

Where the choice exists between operating through a foreign branch or a foreign subsidiary and where the foreign income is exempted abroad in a state not a party to a bilateral treaty, the alternatives are:

For France, Netherlands and the United Kingdom the ultimate choice will depend on the respective advantages afforded by the foreign country. If losses are expected during the first years, a branch abroad might be desirable.

For the United States a foreign subsidiary will normally defer tax at home, but here again the available structures abroad will play their role in the final decision.

In the case of Germany a subsidiary could benefit from the dividend exemption, but a branch operation would be fully taxed in Germany. It should be stressed that the affiliation privilege applies to companies only.

In the case of Belgium there is a definite advantage to operate through a subsidiary instead of a branch as permanent investments are tax free and branch income is subject to full corporate tax.

It is of interest to note that:

The United States and United Kingdom (except for the tax sparing provision in bilateral treaties) investors will not normally be able to receive a permanent benefit from the situation where the foreign income is tax free or tax exempted. Much practical benefit can however be obtained from the defferal of domestic tax and it is to this end that planning is often directed.

On the other hand French, German (only corporations), Dutch and Belgian investors have more flexibility to choose a structure which will preserve the foreign tax advantage and distribute to their shareholders

8. See France page 105.

income which has not been taxed at any stage. This result is achieved in each State through different taxation concepts.

France	:	As a result of the territoriality concept.
Germany	:	As an incentive to invest in developing countries
Belgium	:	Because it is assumed that foreign dividends have been subject to corporate tax abroad.
Holland	:	The income is exempt if it has been subject to a comparable foreign tax regardless of whether the tax has in fact been levied or not and regardless of the rate at which it was levied.

COMPERATIVE TABLE

In order to compare the relative rates suffered by the parent company in the situation of exempt operations income, the following highly simplified table has been prepared; the basic assumption is that 100% of the operating income is distributed.

The qualification provisions for affiliation privilege are different in each investing territory, but in all States except Germany (where 25% participation is required) a long term holding of over 10% would normally qualify. (See table.)

DOMESTIC TAX BURDEN OF FOREIGN EXEMPT INCOME

Country	Domestic tax rate of exempt foreign branch income	Domestic tax rates of foreign exempt dividends received by corporations	
		Dividends from qualifying subsidiaries	Non qualifying dividends
Belgium	48%	effectively Nil[1]	effecitively 33%[2]
France	Nil	effectively 2.25%[3]	50%
Germany	36%[4]	Nil[5]	36%[4]
Netherlands	Nil[6]	Nil[7]	48%
United Kingdom	52%	52%	52%
United States	48%[8]	48%	48%

1. See Belgium page 100.
2. See Belgium page 101.
3. See France page 106.
4. It is assumed that profits will be distributed at a later date and are subject to a global domestic corporate tax burden of 36%.
5. Dividends from developing country subsidiaries are tax exempted in Germany.
6. See Netherlands page 123.
7. See Netherlands page 124.
8. Adjusted profits over $ 50,000.

D. Where Branch Income Is Taxed Abroad

United States

The branch is fully taxable, but overall foreign tax credit is available unless denied by the 'Anti-Boycott' provisions. Unused foreign taxes may be carried back two years and forward five years.

Belgium

Foreign income as adjusted for Belgian tax purposes is subject to the reduced tax rate (12%). Foreign taxes are deductible expenses.

France

Under the territoriality system, foreign income is not included in the taxable base and therefore it is not taxed in France, but no credit is available for foreign taxes paid. Foreign taxes paid are deductible as an expense.

Germany and United Kingdom

The branch income is fully taxable; foreign corporate income taxes are creditable only insofar as they do not exceed German or UK corporation tax on the foreign income as adjusted for German or UK tax purposes. Any excess tax not credited is lost and is not deductible as an expense. In the case of Germany, the Developing Countries Tax Law may be of application.

Netherlands

The unilateral relief measures provide for an exemption of Dutch corporate tax instead of a credit for foreign taxes.

E. Where Subsidiary Income Is Taxed Abroad

United States

In some cases shareholders may be taxed on undistributed foreign income.[9] Tax deferral may be possible.

9. See US page 140.

Overall foreign tax credit is available unless denied by the 'Anti-Boycott' provisions. In some circumstances credit may be claimed for the underlying foreign income taxes paid or accrued on dividends received by a domestic corporation from its foreign subsidiaries through the third tier.

Taxable base is gross foreign income including underlying taxes.

Deduction can be chosen instead of credit.

Unused foreign taxes may be carried back two years and forward five years.

BELGIUM

There are no profit distribution requirements.

Dividends from 'permanent investments' are exempt from Belgian taxation to the extent of 90% or 95% depending upon whether the Belgian company qualifies as a holding company or not. The dividend income to be reported is 105% of the *net* amount received.

The mark up (5%) will be credited against the corporate income tax payable by the receiving corporation and any excess credit is refundable.

Dividends from non-permanent investments are granted a flat foreign tax credit equal to 15% on the *net* amount received.

FRANCE

There are no profit distribution requirements.

If the requirements of Article 39 Octies are fulfilled only 5% of the net amount of dividends remitted is to be included in the French taxable base.

In the subsequent distribution of dividends to the shareholders, a précompte will be assessed because the dividends result from profits which have not borne company tax in France.

Some provisions can be made for losses and investment expenses but these must be recaptured.

GERMANY

In some cases undistributed profits can be subject to German Corporation Tax.[10]

Dividends received by a German corporation from a foreign affiliate or subsidiary (at least 25% participation) are grossed up by the amount of direct and indirect foreign tax paid and are subject to German corporate tax, but a credit may be claimed for the direct and indirect taxes paid.

10. See Germany page 114.

Under the Developing Countries Tax Law deductions can be made for investment expenses, this gives a cash flow advantage, as the amount deducted has to be recaptured at a later date.

If the qualifying foreign dividends originate from an affiliate or subsidiary located in a developing country the indirect foreign tax credit is deemed to be equal to the German Corporation Income Tax on the dividends from such subsidiary or affiliate so that no tax becomes due on such dividends in Germany. This is only the case if dividends are received by a corporation as the affiliation privilege is not applicable to individuals.

Netherlands

There are no profit distribution requirements.

The affiliation privilege has the effect that dividends remitted are not taxed in the Netherlands provided there is a 5% participation and the investment is deemed to be active.

Neither credit nor deduction for foreign taxes is available.

United Kingdom

At least two thirds of the profits of a foreign subsidiary may be required to be remitted under Exchange Control regulations.

In computing the UK tax on foreign income, the net foreign income received is grossed up at the rate of foreign tax. The gross foreign income is then included in the taxable base and the foreign tax is credited, insofar as it does not exceed the UK tax on the gross foreign income.

Foreign tax to be credited includes foreign corporate tax on the profits out of which the dividend is paid.

Excess credit is lost.

F. Summary for Taxable Income

In the absence of bilateral treaties:

Where the profits are to be taxed abroad, the choice between a branch or a subsidiary:

— *For the French or Dutch* investor will depend on the respective advantages granted by the foreign country.
— *For Germany*[11] *and Belgium* the dividend exemption at home is an

11. In this case the dividend exemption applies because all Middle East States in this study are considered to be developing countries.

important advantage for corporate investors, particularly where the foreign tax rates are low.

— *For US and UK* investors, a foreign subsidiary will normally defer domestic tax.

Circumstances arise where theoretically, a foreign subsidiary provides for domestic tax deferral or even tax exemption, but other considerations might lead the international investor to opt for a branch office abroad, these can include the possibility of losses in the early years and a desire to be able to leave a territory with the minimum problems, should conditions deteriorate there; another set of circumstances where a branch structure can be of advantage is where an overall 'turnkey' contract is concerned that is split between:

— selling goods to a foreign port (trade with),
— provision for technical services in the foreign country,
— assembly and manufacture in the foreign country,

and is then the subject of:

— Sales Contracts,
— Service Contracts,
— Joint-Venture Agreements (branches) for industrial activities.

In these circumstances a branch structure tends to have the maximum flexibility and thus facilitates fixing transfer prices (within appropriate limits) that reduce the profit element taxable in the operating State and the overall obligation to the partners in that State.

Each case must be treated individually on its merits and the weight that should be attached to the various key factors carefully assessed.

Example

In the case of Saudi Arabia, a branch or a legal entity (depending on the business field) can be opened without local participation and the profits deemed to be of Saudi source are taxable in the Kingdom. (In the investors countries there may be a tax credit for the taxes paid in the Kingdom e.g. Germany, Japan, US, UK.) However because there are no bilateral treaties with any country, this can result in part of the income being taxed twice as a credit will be granted in the investor country for taxes paid on income deemed to be of foreign source only.

In general terms supply profits should be maximised (especially if they can be earned in intermediate companies) and erection profits minimised; however in striking a quantitative balance in a particular case, the following are amongst the variables that require consideration:

Case of a Saudi branch

No local participation.

Profits are not to be shared but the income is taxable in the Kingdom.

Domestic taxation with credit granted (not always full credit).

In many cases a 100% foreign branch will have marketing disadvantages.

Case of a legal entity without local participation
Same as the branch, but domestic tax aspects may be different.[12]

Case of a legal entity with local participation
Profits are to be shared accordingly.
Taxation in the Kingdom on the foreign share of profits.
Taxation at home with credit.
Marketing advantages will often arise from the introduction of National Capital.

Case of an exempted company (under the Foreign Capital Investment Code)
There will be no taxation in the Kingdom for five years, but in practice 50% local participation appears to be increasingly desirable.
Profits will have to be shared accordingly.
Exempt income may be fully taxable at home without any relief.[13]
Other advantages to be considered in the case of an exempt company are:
— Double taxation problems are avoided;
— The use of a management contract may result in a reallocation of profits;
— In some circumstances investors may not want to pay taxes abroad because they cannot utilise additional foreign tax credit; this is particularly applicable to the United Kingdom and the United States.

Comparative Table

In order to compare relative overall effective rates for the non exempt situation in the country of operations, a number of broad assumptions need to be made:
— Average rate of 40% corporate tax in State of operations;
— Adjusted profit in State of operations and Domestic State are the same;
— In each case the subsidiary is assumed to be qualifying.
On the basis of these assumptions, the position can be illustrated by the following highly simplified table.

12. See Taxation Interactions pages 27-29.
13. See Taxation Interactions pages 28 and 29.

COMPARATIVE GLOBAL TAX BURDEN OF FOREIGN EARNED INCOME

Country	Net dividend after foreign tax [1]	Domestic tax		Foreign tax credit	Total tax burden	
		Branch	Subsidiary		Branch	Subsidiary
Belgium	60	12% on 60 = 7.20[2]	(1.49)[3]	0	47.20%	38.51%
France	60	Nil	2.25[4]		40 %	42.25%
Germany	60	36% on 100 = 36	Nil	36	40 %	40 %
Netherlands	60	Nil	Nil		40 %	40 %
United Kingdom	60	52% on 100 = 52	52% on 100 = 52	40	52 %	52 %
United States	60	48% on 100 = 48	48% on 100 = 48	40	48 %	48 %

1. It is assumed that foreign dividend before tax is 100 and that foreign tax is 40%.
2. See Belgium page 97.
3.

Net dividend after tax	60.00
Notional foreign withholding tax 5% on 60	3.00
Sub Total	63.00
95% deduction on 63	59.85
Subject to corporate tax	3.15
Corporate tax 48% on 3.15	1.51
Credit for Notional foreign withholding tax	3.00
Excess refunded	1.49

4.

Net dividend after foreign tax	60.00
Dividend exemption 95%	57.00
Sub Total	3.00
Précompte 50% on 3	1.50
Subject to corporate tax	4.50
Corporate tax 50% on 4.50	2.25

G. Summary of Important Factors to Consider in the Analysis of a Particular Case

As stressed before the function to the tax planner will be to study and analyse not only the tax legislation and commercial legislation of the foreign territory but also the legislative and fiscal consequences at home. There is set out below a list of important points that should be solved before entering into a specific business operation.

- Comparability of tax
- Relief availability against domestic tax payable on adjusted profits
- Taxes on the amount of rent for business premises
- Contracts with tax reimbursement provisions
- Absence of Tax decree
- Domestic tax consequences of a 'Partnership Structure'
- Exemptions granted on condition that the tax benefit is not to be nullified in the investors own State
- Participation requirements
- Timing of dividends

a) Comparability of tax

In most countries the legislation requires that foreign tax can only be credited if the foreign income has been subject abroad to a tax of a nature similar to the domestic one. As in all the investors' countries considered the corporate tax levied is a tax on the profits, the planner should therefore make sure that the tax levied in the Middle East countries is accepted as comparable. (See the Dutch case cited on page 127.)
Among the investors' countries the United Kingdom is the only one which has published a list of admissible and inadmissible taxes.

If the foreign tax is not considered similar to the domestic corporation tax, it will normally be treated as a deductible expense.

b) Relief is available against domestic tax payable on the adjusted profits

Normally the amount of credit for foreign tax to be allowed against corporation tax is restricted to a maximum of the corporation tax attributable to adjusted profits. In arriving at taxable income in accordance with domestic tax principles there may be adjustments to the taxable income as determined by the foreign country. This can result in part of the tax credit being lost. The tax planner should therefore investigate the extent to which the operating territory's regulations on adjusting profits for tax purposes will differ from that of the investor's own State.

c) Can tax calculated on the amount of rent paid for office premises instead of taxes on income be allowed for foreign tax credit

In many of the United Arab Emirates no taxes on corporate profits are levied, but in lieu a tax on the amount of rent paid for office and domestic premises is paid annually. (See Gulf States page 88.) The issue is to find out if such tax is allowed for foreign tax credit purposes. However in most investors' states such taxes are deductible as expenses rather than as tax credits because they are not considered to be tax on profits.

d) Contracts with tax reimbursement provisions

In a limited number of cases particularly in Saudi Arabia government departments have signed contracts provisions permitting reimbursement by way of contract price adjustment from the government department with which the contract was concluded of the taxes paid to the national fiscal authorities. These cases will require the most careful analysis to establish the status to be granted by the domestic tax authorities to such reimbursement.

e) Absence of Tax decree resulting in tax free income in the Middle East State

In some cases the absence of an income tax decree in the Middle East State may result in a loss of tax exemptions at home (e.g. Holland see page 122.) In these cases an intermediate company may be an appropriate solution to preserve the tax benefit granted by the Middle East State.

f) Domestic tax consequences of 'Partnership' in the Middle East country

In a number of Middle East States and particularly Kuwait and Saudi Arabia a form of partnership can be the only type of entity available in practice to a foreign investor.

In most cases such 'Partnerships' which in Kuwait and Saudi Arabia have statutes very similar to that of a French 'Société à responsabilité Limité' ('SARL') will be regarded as corporate entities in the Investing countries; this does not however, hold good for all cases and in some investor states such as the US the tax status will be determined by the precise terms of the formation documents.

The most careful consideration therefore requires to be given to the status of a particular proposed partnership in the investor's own country *prior* to the finalisation of the formation documents.

g) Case where tax exemptions are granted in the Middle East State on the condition that the tax benefit is not lost domestically

If such is the case (example Egypt) the tax planner will have to use an intermediate company located in a tax haven, or possibly in a country exempting under specific circumstances income from developing countries (Germany) or exempting in some cases foreign source income (Holland).

Chapter VI
Tax Havens and Intermediate Companies

Use of Intermediate Companies

a) If the foreign investor is involved in activities in the Middle East States where tax is not levied intermediate holding companies can sometimes be used to retain part of the tax benefits granted in the Middle East or alternatively to create an element of tax deferral.

b) Non controlled intermediate companies may also be used to protect American investors against the new 'Anti Boycott' regulations but investors should be careful that such procedures are not nullified by anti-avoidance legislation.

c) In most Middle East countries defining the extent of taxable income involves consideration of the classic distinction between trading 'in a territory' and trading 'with a territory'. In view of this it is important to ensure that the relative value of the supply component of any contract is identified clearly in the contractual documents and many contractors arrange for a separate affiliate to be responsible for the supply element. The supply affiliate can sometimes be located in a low or nil tax intermediate state and create an element of tax deferral in relation to profits allocated to it.

d) In one particular case (Egypt — non free zone companies) tax exemptions are granted 'only as long as profits are not subject to taxation in the investors' home country'. In the light of this investors often hold their participation via a holding company in a country where foreign source income is not taxable.

It can therefore, be concluded that the basic purpose of intermediate companies in the investment context is to seek to preserve the tax advantages granted to foreign operations in the countries analysed in this study; in many cases the preservation takes the form of a deferral from home country taxes rather than an absolute benefit.

The main requirements are that the intermediate company is located in a country which can offer the following:

— Favourable treatment of foreign source income (branch income and dividends),
— No exchange control constraints on cross financing operations,
— Possibility to finance overseas operations through Eurocurrency borrowings,
— Low incorporation fees, lack of onerous incorporation formalities and speed of incorporation,
— Freedom of commercial action,
— Political stability,
— Existence of communications and service infrastructure,
— The benefits of treaties.

Possible Tax Haven locations can be classified into the following basic categories:
— Nil tax,
— Nil tax activities outside the Haven,
— Low Tax,
— Special exemptions for particular types of foreign source income.

Some countries encouraging the establishment of intermediate holding companies which are often convenient for use in connection with Middle East Operations are:
— Bermuda,
— Panama,
— Liberia.

In the case of Bermuda which is a nil tax state, a special class of holding or Exempt Company is created which cannot engage in domestic commercial, or industrial activity.

An alternative approach used in Panama and Liberia is the exemption from corporate taxation of foreign source income accruing to the tax haven company.

A. Bermuda

Taxation

There is no taxation in Bermuda by way of taxes on profits, dividends or income and neither is there any capital gains tax, gift tax or estate duty. Similarly, the salary of an individual does not attract taxation. There is, however, an Employment Tax but this does not apply to exempted companies unless they have a licence to trade in Bermuda. The only form of tax imposed on an exempted company or partnership is an annual fee of BD $ 650[1] except in the case of companies writing insurance or reinsurance as principal mutual fund business or raising money from the public, where the annual fee is BD $ 1,000.[1]

1. To be increased to BD $ 800 and 1,500 respectively on 1st January 1978.

In addition, an exempted company can, under the Exempted Undertakings Tax Protection Act 1966, apply for an undertaking from the Government that in the event that taxation is introduced it will not be applicable to that exempted company until 29th March 2006.

Exchange Control

In June 1972 Bermuda ceased to be part of the Sterling Area and by the Exchange Control Act of 29th June 1972 Bermuda became a currency area of its own so that all other countries in the world and other currencies are now external so far as Bermuda is concerned. This means that an exempted company may trade and maintain bank accounts in any currency if it so desires and it is completely free to remit or repatriate such funds.

However, accounts in Bermuda Dollars may only be maintained to defray normal local expenses.

Others

- Capital must be fully subscribed but need not be fully paid up.
- An exempted company is obliged to maintain its registered office in Bermuda.

B. PANAMA

As stated before, the income tax law in Panama is based on the 'territoriality' concept, this means that income derived from transactions outside the country are tax exempted.

Income Tax Law

The law defines the activities which are not subject to Panama income tax which include foreign source income accruing to foreign shareholders in Panama corporations. (Mainly invoicing of merchandise handled abroad, distribution of dividends, management of foreign operations).

Exchange Control

Panama has no exchange control. There is no tax on transfer of funds of any nature and no restrictions on the movements of funds.

Other

Directors can be non-residents in Panama, but every company must have an attorney as *resident* agent.

C. Liberia

The taxation and exchange control positions can be summarised as follows:

Taxation

If more than 50% of the shares of a Liberian corporation are held by non-Liberians, then all foreign source income is exempt from income tax.

Dividend payments to non-residents are exempted from withholding tax.

Exchange Control

There is no exchange control whatsoever.

Other

— Directors and shareholders may reside anywhere.
— Minimum capital requirement is $ 500.

D. Low Taxes on Holding Companies: The Netherlands Antilles

Some tax havens impose tax at very low rather than nil rates and this can be useful in certain circumstances. This is the case when no tax decree is issued in the Middele East State and when the investor's country exempts the foreign income on the condition it was subject to tax abroad.

Among the low tax havens the Netherlands Antilles is of particular interest:

— Investment and holding companies receiving income from outside the Netherlands Antilles are subject to tax at a very low rate of 2.4% on adjusted profits not exceeding NAFl 100.000 ($ 40.000) and of 3% on profits above this figure.
— No surtax is payable nor are capital gains taxable.
— There is no withholding tax on dividends or interests.
— There is an initial commercial registration fee and an annual fee both related to the amount of paid up capital.
— The Netherlands Antilles have double taxation agreements with the Netherlands, Surinam, the USA, the UK, Denmark and Norway.
— Investment companies and special holding companies operating on behalf of non residents and not engaged in local business can be licensed to transfer capital and income abroad without requiring prior approval of the Foreign Exchange Control Board.
— To benefit from the tax advantages a limited liability company formed

under the laws of the Netherlands Antilles is required, (very similar to Dutch law). The founders can be natural or legal persons, the act of incorporation can be done by proxy and no local director is required.

E. Special Exemptions for Particular Types of Foreign Source Income

A number of high tax countries can be used for tax deferral purposes in special circumstances. In that context the Netherlands have become a haven for certain holding companies and in recent years much use has been made of Dutch intermediary companies for Middle East operations. The basic advantages of Holland over a pure tax haven are:

- Respectability in that Holland is not normally regarded as a haven by Middle East government agencies;
- Access to a comprehensive network of treaties;
- The ability to use Holland as a European coordinating centre;
- Holland is often a good location for joint ventures because of the tax situation of European partners in such joint ventures.

The basic conditions that must be fulfilled if income or participation dividends are to be exempted from income tax in Holland are:

Participation Dividends

- The Dutch recipient company must hold at least 5% of the equity share capital of a foreign corporation.
- The foreign company must have been subject to a tax comparable with Dutch tax on income. (In determining comparability withholding taxes on dividends are ignored.)
- The Dutch company must hold the participation from the beginning of (the Dutch company's) fiscal year in which a distribution is made.
- The participation must be held for a business related purpose and not for investment purposes.
- The distributing entity must be a non-resident company and not an investment trust.

Foreign Source Income

- The existence of a bona-fide permanent establishment in the foreign country;
- The foreign source income must have been subject to a tax comparable with Dutch tax on income.

The use of Holland is unquestionably more complex than a traditional haven and the following matters require close consideration:

The condition of being subject to a 'comparable' foreign tax on income: In a number of cases (Dubai or Sharjah), the foreign company or branch has not in fact paid tax because the applicable decree has not been enforced; in principle however branch profits or dividends 'have been subject to tax' and will not therefore be taxed in Holland.

If there is any doubt, a written clearance should be obtained from the Dutch fiscal authorities.

No exemption due to timing of dividend payment: It is important to plan the timing of dividends to ensure that the Dutch company holds a participation from the beginning of a fiscal year in which a dividend is to be paid.

Non-comparability of foreign tax: This has given rise to questions particularly in the case of Saudi Arabia; a written clearance should be obtained in cases of doubt.

F. Competitive Havens in the Middle East

The Middle East has not had a traditional multipurpose tax haven, although, because of the application of the territoriality principle (which exempts the non-Lebanese activities of Lebanese companies from Lebanese corporate tax), Lebanon has often been used as a partial haven, particularly for distribution activities. Its position was improved by the favourable terms of its double tax treaty with France.

Given that commercial activity and confidence generally in Lebanon is likely to take a considerable time to recover from its recent political problems, the practical choices of Middle East Haven territories are:

Sharjah, Ajman and Ras Al-Khaimah

Until recently it was possible for wholly foreign interests to incorporate (by Amir's Charter) in anyone of the Emirates and for the Company thus incorporated to be entirely tax free. This is however no longer possible in either Abu Dhabi or Dubai but it remains possible in the other Emirates.

Of these Sharjah, Ajman and Ras Al-Khaimah are of immediate interest as possible locations for tax haven companies; the two remaining Emirates Umm Al-Qawain and Fujeirah are also possible locations, but do not as yet have the commercial infrastructure and communications facilities that are required.

Tax haven companies appear to have been actually formed in these

Emirates but the Governments tend to favour those carrying out bona-fide commercial activity in the Emirate in addition to acting as a nil tax holding company.

Sharjah has announced that it is studying the enactment of a comprehensive company law and that it may bring in at the same time a low tax of (say) 1% on both corporate and (possibly) also the personal income of Sharjah residents.

Bahrain

Another territory with tax haven potential is Bahrain which has at present no corporate or personal taxes. The Government has been reported to be considering an 'offshore' company law[2] and has already licensed a class of Offshore Banks; the latter can be wholly non-Bahraini controlled are not at present subject to taxation and pay a flat fee of US $25,000 to the Bahrain Monetary Agency for the operating license.

2. Legislation was introduced in November 1977.

Part II
The Operating Territories

Introduction

The purpose of this part is to summarize the basic principles that the State of operation applies to the foreign company wishing to carry on business in its territory.

The chapters on each jurisdiction follow a common basic pattern and in addition introduce special features where these are likely to be of particular significance.

The common pattern is:

— Basic principles of taxing foreign business activity,
— Taxes and tax rates applicable to foreign business activity,
— Computation of Taxable income,
— Incentive legislation,
— Corporate Entities Available,
— Formation Procedures,
— Taxation Treaties,
— Exchange Control.

Additional sections have been added in relation to particular countries wherever this seems justified.

When using the information contained in this section it must, however, be emphasised that many of the States concerned interpret the legislation with a wide degree of administrative discretion, and it will often be desirable to review the facts of a particular case with the officials concerned, prior to entering into a commitment.

It should also be borne in mind that both law and adminstrative practice are subject to change; this is particularly pertinent in relation to Egypt and the Sudan where tax reforms are currently in progress. The information given relates to June 1977 (unless otherwise stated) and therefore requires to be checked in the light of law and practice at the time a decision is taken.

In the course of this section (and also in Part I) the US Dollar has been used as a unit of comparison. The following exchange rates have been applied which approximate to those ruling as at 30th June 1977:

State	*Currency Unit*	*Abbreviation*	*Rate in terms of US $*
Bahrain	Bahrain Dinar	BD	2.53
Egypt	Egyptian Pound	£E	1.43[1]
Iraq	Iraq Dinar	ID	3.45
Kuwait	Kuwait Dinar	KD	3.48
Oman	Oman Riyal	OR	2.89
Qatar	Qatar Riyal	QR	0.253
Saudi Arabia	Saudi Riyal	SR	0.283
Sudan	Sudan Pound	£S	2.49[2]
United Arab Emirates	UAE Dirham	DH	0.256

1. The rate in the official parallel market
2. The official rate after considering the 15% incentive for convertible currencies purchasing £S.

At the end of the section there is set out a list of the principal relevant statutes in the operating territories considered.

Chapter I
Egypt

Companies

A. Basic Principles

Companies registered in Egypt, branches of foreign companies and commercial partnerships are subject to Egyptian taxes on their income derived from sources in Egypt. The tax system is schedular although certain income may be assessed under more than one schedule, but will be subject to partial relief against taxes imposed under another over-riding schedule. It is therefore essential in considering Egyptian tax matter to have regard to the incidence of tax on a particular source of income.

B. Taxes and Tax Rates

The following being the principal direct taxes on companies are described below:
— Tax on Commercial Profits
— Tax on Income from Movable Property
— Tax on Interest

Tax on Commercial Profits

This tax is charged on companies registered in Egypt, branches of foreign companies and commercial partnerships (defined to exclude professional partnerships) and can be regarded as a tax on undistributed profits, as it is assessed only on the balance of taxable income after deduction of dividends paid in respect of the year. Accordingly, although branches of foreign corporations are subject to this tax, there is no assessment in practice as their profits are deemed to be fully distributed by way of dividend to the foreign parent.

The effective rate of tax on corporate profits is at present 39.7%, made up as follows (the taxes other than profit tax are assessed on the same profits):

	Rate %
Profit Tax	17.0
Defence Tax	10.5
National Security Tax	8.0
War Tax	2.5
Municipality Tax	1.7
Total rate %	39.7

Tax on Income from Movable Property

This tax is charged on the distributed profits of Egyptian corporations, branches and partnerships and certain other types of income which are summarised as follows:

— Interest and dividends on bonds, shares and securities of Egyptian companies,
— Scrip or specie dividends,
— Interest on loans,
— Directors remuneration (except for up to two whole time service directors' remuneration to a maximum of £E 3,000 per annum each),
— Interest and dividends received from foreign securities and remitted to Egypt (after deducting any foreign tax paid on an expense basis),
— Net profits, as computed for the tax on commercial profits of branches of foreign corporations.

The following are exempt from the tax on movable property.[1] Dividends paid by an investment company (defined as a company of which 90% of capital, reserves and loans are invested in securities, bonds and shares) to the extent that they are matched by income received under deduction of tax from movable property. Dividends paid by an Egyptian Holding company to the extent that they are matched by dividends received under deduction of tax from other Egyptian and foreign companies.

The rate of tax on income derived from movable property is at present 40.55%, made up as follows. (The taxes other than the tax on movable property are assessed on the same profits).

	Rate %
Tax on income from movable property	17.00
Defence Tax	10.50
National Security Tax	8.00
War Tax	2.50
Municipality Tax	2.55
Total rate %	40.55

1. Article 36 Income tax law 14 of 1939 as amended.

Tax on interest

This tax is charged (and collected by deduction) in respect of interest accruing from Egyptian sources including interest on capital invested in Egypt and paid to non-residents. Interest paid to individuals or companies resident in Egypt from non-resident sources is also chargeable.

The tax is charged on all interest arising from mortgages, debts and deposits except interest arising in respect of business loans or deposits, which is subject to the tax on commercial profits; it must be deducted at source in all cases except when the interest is payable to a bank, credit institution or joint stock company with its head office in Egypt.

The present effective rate of tax is 40.55% and has the same components as the tax on income derived from movable property. The tax is, however, paid by deduction at source and the payer must account for deductions to the Fiscal Administration by the 15th of the month following the month of payment.

As from 1st May 1977 it is not levied on Egyptian source Bank Deposit Income.

C. Computation of Taxable Income

Taxable profits and losses are based on the trading results shown by the financial accounts prepared for statutory purposes but adjusted, inter alia, in respect of the following:

— The charge for depreciation must be adjusted to the annual rates which have been approved by the Fiscal Administration:

Buildings	2 – 2 1/2%
Trucks	20%
Office Machinery	15%
Office & Shop Furniture	6%
Plant & Machinery	10% – 30% (depending on category and use)

— Profits or losses on the disposal of fixed assets are included as trading income.

— 90% of any income which has been subjected to or exempted from the tax on movable property is deductible.

— The annual rental value of premises owned by the taxpayer is also deducted as this will be assessed to property tax.

— Losses may be carried forward and utilized against taxable profits arising in any of the three subsequent financial years.

— Provisions for bad debts are not allowed unless a court order has been obtained for the debts. All other general provisions are disallowed.

D. Incentive Legislation

These have been granted by Law No. 43 for 1974 and apply primarily to non-Egyptian Investors (Arab or Non-Arab) in Egypt.

a) Free Zone projects

Free zones have been designed as tax havens not subject to the exchange controls and customs duties of Egypt with the object of stimulating investment in specific 'territorial' areas.

Free zones are either areas designated by the Egyptian Government in Port Said, Suez, Ismalia and Alexandria or other areas chosen by foreign investors and accepted by the authority as enjoying the same concessions. The principal concessions are as follows:

1) Exemptions from all exchange controls
2) Indefinite exemption from corporate income tax and divided tax.
3) Foreign employees exemption from the general tax on income and death duties.
4) Exemption from customs duties and import restrictions.

The only levy is 1% on the arms-length invoiced value of goods imported and exported if goods are being produced or a negotiated rate not to exceed 3% on value added in the case of a Service Industry.

No local participation is required in a free zone project.

b) Non-Free Zone projects

Non free zone projects receive the benefit of exemption from taxation and from certain exchange control regulations in return for a substantial investment in Egypt. In order to qualify for the various exemptions an investment has to be made in one of the following fields:

- Industry,
- Mining,
- Energy,
- Tourism,
- Transportation,
- Land Reclamation,
- Cattle Production Development,
- Water Resources,
- Housing Projects and related projects,
- Investment companies which employ capital in the fields stipulated in this law,
- Investment banks and trading banks and re-insurance companies which deal only in foreign currencies,
- Banks which can conduct operations in local currency having at least a 51% majority of Egyptian equity capital,

— Construction and rehabilitation activities in regions outside the agricultural area and the perimeters of existing cities,
— Contracting activities undertaken by Joint Stock companies in which there is at least 50 percent participation of Egyptian Capital,
— Technical consulting activities in the form of a Joint Stock company in partnership with a foreign international consultant.

In general, priority will be given to projects which develop exports or tourism or reduce the need for import of essential goods together with projects which require technical qualifications or the use of patents and/or other exclusive Industrial Property.

Non free zone projects must operate with Egyptian public or private participation. The requirements for the participation of Arab or Egyptian National capital can be summarised as follows:
— Any foreign capital in Housing Projects must be Arab capital. It is understood that an executive decision made in August 1975 restricts any foreign capital to leasing the land used in small projects.
— Investment Banks and Trading Banks can be wholly owned by either foreign or Arab capital if their activities are limited to operations executed in foreign currencies.
— Other projects can be wholly owned by either foreign or Arab capital, but only provided a 2/3 majority vote of agreement is obtained from the Authority. This is rarely given and in practice Egyptian equity participation must be at least 25%.

Non free zone projects are granted an exemption from all direct taxes on industrial profits and 'the taxes appendant thereto' for five years commencing from the tax year in which the project becomes operational. The exemption may in certain circumstances be extended to eight years.

It is important for a foreign investor to carefully consider the terms of Article 16 of law 43 which states that: 'These exemptions shall remain applicable only as long as the profits of the project are not, as a consequence, subject to taxation in the foreign investor's home country or in any other country.'

Although practice on this matter is not yet clear, it is believed that the authorities will not regard as 'taxation' capital taxation primarily calculated by reference to net worth such as is levied on Luxembourg holding companies.

It is also suggested that no taxation would have arisen on the profits if the project of a parent company to whom dividends were paid by a law 43 company subsequently incurred withholding tax on paying its retained profits to its members.

Having regard to the above it is clearly most important for a prospective foreign Investor to carefully examine the double taxation position that will arise in the specific circumstances contemplated and, where appropriate, seek a ruling from the Egyptian or foreign taxation authorities involved.

The following further taxation points should be noted:

- The tax exemption does not extend to Royalties, Management fees and technical assistance payments made to both Egyptians and non-Egyptian entities;
- After the holiday has expired up to 5 percent of the equity capital held by an individual is exempt from the general tax on income;
- Expatriates employed by non free zone companies are exempt from the general tax on income.

E. Corporate Entities Available

The principal forms of structure likely to be attractive to the investor are:

a) Branch: From the fiscal point of view it is convenient that a branch structure be adopted in the early stages before the production has been launched as there is likely to be a fiscal loss in at least part of this period which might be available for relief against any head office profits. It is also likely to be helpful from the practical point of view in that the formalities for establishing a branch are rather simpler than those required to establish a Law 43 non free zone company;

b) A Law 43 company in the free zone;

c) A Law 43 company not in the free zone.

In a) and c) the law permits several types of corporate structure in particular, a 'Limited Liability Partnership' or a 'Joint Stock Company'. Under Law 43 of 1974 requirements concerning the number of partners, board of directors, statutes are slightly different from the normal commercial law (example: a joint stock company may be established with less than seven shareholders).

F. Formation Procedures

a) Branch

The establishment of a branch would entail the submission of certain information and documents to the Egyptian Commercial Registry, details of which are as follows:

- Legal form of the Company,
- Name under which it trades,
- Objects,
- Date of formation and duration of the Company,
- Issued and paid up capital,
- Nominal value of the shares,
- Names, dates of birth and nationality of the members of the Board of Directors,

—Name, date of birth, and nationality of the manager of the branch.

No specific amount of capital is required for a branch. The registration of a branch would, however, usually require proof of transfer to Egypt of at least EL 5,000.

The manager of the branch in Egypt may either be an Egyptian or a foreign national.

Once a branch is established, it is subject to the Egyptian laws, and particularly the following laws:

—The Companies Law,
—The Labour Laws,
—The Exchange Control Law and Regulations,
—The Tax Laws.

b) A Law 43 Company in the Free Zone

A licence must be obtained within one month from the Board of the particular free zone after approval for a project has been obtained from the Board of Authority for the foreign investor and financial deposits made of not less than LE 500.[2] Licences are initially granted for a period of 25 years. At the end of the period of the licence all machinery and buildings should be removed if the land is rented from the Authority unless the management of the free zone asks to buy them. If land has been purchased it can be sold to a new licencee.

No manufacturing, construction or producing is necessarily required by the Law in order to operate in one of these areas which contrasts with a non free zone investment under Law 43.

All free zone projects must provide training for unskilled Egyptian Labour 'in order that they may become skilled'.[3] The proportion of personnel having Egyptian nationality must not be less than 75%.

c) A Law 43 Company in a Non Free Zone

There are currently no requirements as to the form of legal entity the project takes (i.e. company, branch, partnership), but a standard form of articles and memorandum for a free zone company has now been issued by the Authority and non-free zone companies must normally comply with this.

G. Taxation Treaties

Among the investor's countries considered in this Study Egypt has concluded a tax treaty with Germany, Japan, and the United States (not yet ratified).

2. Articles 73 to 76 Decree 91.
3. Article 54 Law 43.

Although there are differences in detail a common feature is the retention of the right by Egypt to impose corporate taxes on income attributable to a permanent establishment of the foreign investor located in Egypt and vice versa.

All three treaties mention that no profits shall be attributed to a permanent establishment by reason of the mere purchase by that permanent establishment of goods or merchandise from the parent company.

As far as dividends are concerned each country is entitled to tax within specified limits.

The treaty between the United States and Egypt was signed October 28, 1975 but is not yet ratified. The treaty is drawn along the same lines, but is more explicit on key issues such as the factors to determine whether income is effectively connected with a permanent establishment.

H. Foreign Exchange and Money Control

In the Free Zone

Transactions carried out in a free zone, between free zones or with other countries are not subject to the Egyptian exchange control laws. All receipts and payments, must, therefore be made in foreign currencies. An investor will, however, have to open a special account in Egyptian Pounds called 'The Operations Account', the minimum balance of which must be not less than two months' operations costs. Law 43 provides that this must be supplied by exchanging foreign currency at the official rate[4], but this was amended as from 7th June 1977 by a decree stating that all capital transactions are to be carried out at the incentive rate.

In the Non-Free Zone

The provisions of the law relating to exchange control outside the free zone are complex and subject to administrative discretion. The basic principles are, however, understood to be:

Companies generating foreign currency from exports are allowed to keep their earnings in foreign currency and use it for any of the following matters:

—Transfer of profit,
—Import of raw materials,
—Repayment of loans and/or interest thereon,
—Payment for other services necessary for the projects that have been incurred in foreign currency.

No specific authorisations are required for the above.

4. Article 49 Law 43.

Projects agreed by the authority to be of 'major economic value' and not orientated towards exports can remit abroad the whole of their net profits, the foreign currency to be provided by the Government.

The capital invested in the project (which is defined to include intangible assets at fair market transfer prices) can be repatriated in five annual instalments, after dissolution.

Chapter II
Iraq

Companies

A. Basic Principles

Resident corporate entities (companies incorporated under Iraqi law or other laws and having their place of business or management or control in Iraq) are subject to tax liability in Iraq on income from both domestic and foreign sources, as defined by the income tax regulations. Foreign income is subject to tax even if that income is not received in Iraq.

Non-resident corporate entities are subject to corporate tax on income arising from corporate activity in Iraq.

Partnerships comprising associations of two or more persons in any business activity without registration are not considered to be separate entities for taxation purposes; these are not subject to corporation income, but the partners are assessed directly to personal income tax.

B. Tax Rates

Rates of taxation can vary according to the nature of the taxable entity and it is therefore essential to ascertain the status of a taxable corporate body in Iraq before its taxation position can be determined.

The rates vary from 15% for income under 500 Iraqi Dinars (some $1,700) to 60% for income over 15,000 Iraqi Dinars (some $50,000). The current rates are as follows:

Payable on Taxable Profits		*Types of Taxable Entity Rates are in Percentage*		
	US Dollars	(a)	(b and c)	(d)
Up to	$ 1,695	15	15	15
From	$ 1,696 to $ 3,390	15	15	15
From	$ 3,391 to $ 5,085	20	20	20
From	$ 5,086 to $ 6,780	20	20	20

Payable on Taxable Profits				*Types of Taxable Entity Rates are in Percentage*		
	US Dollars			(a)	(b and c)	(d)
From	$ 6,781	to	$ 8,475	20	20	20
From	$ 8,476	to	$ 10,170	20	20	20
From	$ 10,171	to	$ 13,560	25	25	25
From	$ 13,561	to	$ 16,950	30	30	30
From	$ 16,951	to	$ 20,340	35	35	35
From	$ 20,341	to	$ 23,730	40	40	40
From	$ 23,731	to	$ 27,120	40	40	40
From	$ 27,121	to	$ 30,510	45	45	45
From	$ 30,511	to	$ 33,900	45	45	45
From	$ 33,901	to	$ 37,290	50	50	50
From	$ 37,291	to	$ 40,680	50	50	50
From	$ 40,681	to	$ 50,850	50	55	55
From	$ 50,851			50	55	60

Note

The categories of taxable entities can be broadly distinguished as follows:

a) Public Industrial Company
b) Public Non-industrial Company
c) Private Industrial Company
d) Private Non-industrial Company.

In determining whether a foreign branch is public or private, the basic test appears to be the status of the ultimate holding company.

C. Other Taxes

a) Capital Gains

There is no capital gains tax on companies.

b) Withholding Taxes

Dividends paid by a company out of income on which tax has been paid are not taxed again on distribution. Exchange controls may however limit distributions outside Iraq. (See Exchange Control page 67.)

Interest paid to non-resident banks is subject to a withholding tax of 20% which is not deductible in the computations of the paying company. It will be noted however that in most cases banks will protect themselves in the loan agreement from the effect of this deduction and the liability will thus be effectively borne by the borrower.

c) Other Taxes

Owners or charterers of sea, river, land and air means of transport, residing outside Iraq are liable to tax at a rate of $7^1/_2\%$ of the total amount receivable from passengers, mail, livestock and goods transported *in Iraq.*

d) Patents – Royalties

The position as to the withholding of the taxes on royalties is complex and the taxation treatment afforded is understood to vary considerably. It is recommended, therefore, that specific clearance be obtained as to the treatment the authorities intend to afford to each individual case before an agreement is completed.

D. Computation of Taxable Income

Taxable profits and losses are based on the trading results shown by the financial accounts adjusted for tax purposes. The adjustments include the following:

a) Depreciation at the following annual rates computed on written down value:

Machinery	25%
Contractors' Equipment	30%
Motor Vehicles	20%
Furniture	10%
Buildings	3%

If depreciation is computed on a straight-line basis, only 50% of the above rates are deductible.

b) Profits arising on the sale of fixed assets (written down on either of the acceptable bases mentioned above) are not taxable, nor is relief available for losses.

c) Contractors engaged on contracts for the supply and erection of equipment on which they utilise imported self-manufactured equipment must charge the cost to the contract accounts at arm's length price. The tax authorities will require the addition of a notional profit (normally between 5% to 10% of the billing price) to taxable profits of the contract of the year in which the equipment is imported. Contracts for the supply of equipment only are not subject to this treatment.

d) Trading losses may not be carried back, but can be carried forward against profits for five years, but may be utilised only as to 50% of the taxable profits in each year.

e) The authorities accept that in the case of contracts covering a period of years, it is necessary in drawing up accounts of interim years to make subjective judgments as to the expected out-turn of the contract. They are therefore prepared to accept annual accounts incorporating work in progress at cost plus overheads (computed on a full absorption basis). The overall contract profit is apportioned to individual years on completion of the contract, normally by reference to costs incurred in each year. Certain contracts are exempted from tax by the Development Project Law (see page 67) and others may be taken on a reimbursible basis — that is to say the tendering authority will retrospectively increase the tender price by the amount of tax paid in respect of the Iraqi branch in relation to the contract; foreign firms accepting contracts on this basis will need to give careful consideration to the international taxation implications of this arrangement on their company or group as a whole.

E. Payments to Non-Residents

Management charges by head offices of foreign companies must be supported by detailed justification and be accepted as being on an arm's length basis. In some cases a 'percentage' basis is acceptable to the taxation authorities.

Royalties or technical assistance fees must be the subject of a detailed contract and be approved by various government departments including the Central Bank.

F. Corporate Entities Available

Unless it is contemplated that approved other Arab capital is likely to be involved, a foreign organisation operating in Iraq is likely to be virtually compelled to adopt branch form as a minority holding in a company that has relatively high taxation and severe exchange control restrictions will not normally be attractive. The adoption of branch structure, however can have adverse tax consequences and, in some cases where the major development project legislation exempts the bulk of a branch's activity from Iraqi tax, the benefit can be substantially eroded by taxation of the branch profits in the contractor's own country.

The most careful consideration, therefore, requires to be given to this aspect and wherever possible, interests in Iraqi branches should be routed through countries which exempt branch profits earned outside the territory.

.G. Formation Procedures

a) Documents to be produced to register a foreign branch

- A notarised copy of the Statutes of the company and a certificate of its establishment or other similar document establishing the existance of the company
- The full address of the company's head office
- A list of the company's branches throughout the world
- A list of the names of the company's Board of Directors
- A list of the names of the persons authorised to manage the branch in Iraq and their full address in Iraq, together with a Power of Attorney authorising them to manage the branch in Iraq
- The complete address of the company's branch in Iraq, a notarised affadavit in respect of the absence of relations with Israel, a notarised certificate of reciprocity
- A certificate from the appropriate Government Department that the company has a contract in Iraq or the company is a subcontractor of another company which has such a contract
- Copies of the company's balance sheets for the last three years

b) Procedures

The application must be submitted by an authorised Iraqi lawyer who has been duly appointed with a notarised Power of Attorney.

All the documents must be formally legalised by all of the institutions set out below:
- Official sources in the country where the company is incorporated,
- The Iraqi Embassy or representative in that country,
- Ministry of Foreign Affairs, Iraq,
- Central Bank of Iraq, Baghdad,
- Income Tax Department, Baghdad,
- Court of Cassation, Baghdad,
- Ministry of Justice, Iraq.

Between one and two months should be allowed to complete these procedures.

A company operating through a branch must submit annually balance sheets of itself and the branch to the registrar of companies. Any changes in the Board of Directors or Articles of Association must also be notified within six months of the year end.

H. Incentive Legislation

Iraq has not set out to attract foreign capital in view of its strong payments position, but has introduced legislation (Law No. 157 for 1973) which is designed to facilitate duly registered foreign branches engaged in work relating to major development projects. The definition of 'major development' is an opinion (supported by a written statement) of the public authority supervising the project involved. It is understood that most of the contracts now being put up for international tender are likely to fall into this category. The following summarises the principal benefits that arise in the event the project is accepted as having major development status:

- Exemption from income tax, customs and excise duties and other taxes or dues,
- Exemption from the restrictions on the employment of foreign labour,
- Exemption from import restrictions,
- Temporary exemption from customs duties subject to a personal undertaking (in practice likely to be required from the agent or other authorised representative) for all machinery and equipment used in the project until the issue of a final delivery certificate,
- Exemption from the provisions of Law 39 for 1971 which relates to the social security and leaving indemnities to which the local staff are entitled. The authority supervising the tender takes over the liability provided the contractor keeps proper records and prepares the returns normally required from non-exempt employers.

Notwithstanding the general philosophy of fiscal exemption accorded to approved projects, it should be noted that no exchange control exemptions are available nor are there any personal taxation benefits for the employees (both foreign and local) engaged on the project.

I. Taxation Treaties

Iraq does not, at present, have a double taxation agreement with any other country.

J. Foreign Exchange and Money Control

There is a comprehensive system of controls in force which basically prohibits the export of all funds other than capital of foreign origin or the permitted margin of profit earned thereon.

The calculation of permitted margin will normally arise in practice in the case of foreign participations in Iraqi companies as foreign branches cannot freely remit profits arising on the Iraqi Dinar element of their profits.

For the purposes of the calculation the foreign participation is classified between industrial and non-industrial capital according to the type of Iraqi company involved.

In the case of industrial capital, the margin is the lower of 20% of the paid up capital and reinvested surplus, and the tax adjusted profit after tax of the year to which the remittance relates. For non-industrial companies the permitted percentage is 10%.

Foreign contractors normally seek to overcome the difficulty caused by the fact that a branch does not have paid up capital by stipulating that a proportion of the tender price be paid in foreign currency. It is clearly a matter of competitive judgment how large this proportion should be as the Tendering Authority (usually an Iraq Government agency) will itself have to obtain exchange control approval for the foreign currency stipulated in the tender; in view, however, of the improved position of the Iraqi Dinar following the increase in the price of oil, the percentage of exchange required is now significantly less important than has been the case in recent years.

Chapter III
Saudi Arabia

Companies

A. Basic Principles

Non Saudi companies operating inside the Kingdom or inside and outside the Kingdom simultaneously are chargeable on their Saudi source income to company income tax.[1]

Saudi companies whose capital, partners and share holders are entirely Saudi are not liable to corporate income tax but are liable to Zakat.

Only Saudi Nationals and Saudi firms are subject to the Zakat. Non-Saudis have no right to request substitutions of this levy for other types of taxes. The Zakat is due on the working capital that has been retained for one year, and is charged at the rate of 2.5%. However, recently Royal Decree allowed individuals to pay half of the Zakat to the Government and the other half to be paid to poor persons in accordance with the discretion of the contributors. The principles of this type of levy and its application are determined by the Islamic Law (Shari'a).

Citizens of Bahrain, Kuwait, Qatar are similarly not liable to corporate tax but are liable to Zakat.

B. Tax Rates

The current rates of corporate tax are as follows:

	SR	*US $*	
On the first	100,000	30,000	25%
On the next	400,000	120,000	35%
On the next	500,000	150,000	40%
On profits exceeding	1,000,000	300,000	45%

1. Article 1 Royal Decree 17 — 2 28-576.

Example

If global profits are $320,000 and participation percentages are 50% foreign, 50% Saudi, $160,000 will be subject to income tax at following rates:

	Income		*Tax*
	$ 30,000	25%	$ 7,500
	$ 120,000	35%	$ 42,000
	$ 10,000	40%	$ 4,000
Total	$ 160,000		$ 53,500

C. Other Taxes

Capital Gains

Capital gains arising from sale of real estate, assets, shares, securities are added to the normal trading profits and taxed as business profits at the same rates.

Withholding Taxes

There are no withholding taxes on dividends. Payments to non-residents, including interest and royalties, may, however, become liable to Saudi taxation under the provisions discussed in E page 72.

D. Computation of Taxable Income

The taxable profits or losses are based on the results shown by the financial accounts as adjusted for taxation purposes. The adjustments include the following:

a) Disallowance of expenditure not incurred to acquire or retain taxable income or undocumented expenditure.

b) Disallowance of indirect expenditures:
- No allowances are permitted for head office overheads;
- There is no deduction in respect of publicity expenditure abroad or of any branch management which is not locally based;
- Allowances for expenses incurred abroad are restricted to technical expenses provided that they are fully documented. Technical expenses

2. Circular 3 of 1389.

are defined as the expenses related to 'engineering works of any kind, or to chemical or geological research, or to industrial works'.

c) Contributions and aids paid to the government, charitable organizations and institutions for social welfare which are recognised by the Saudi Arabian Government are deductible but there is no deduction for contributions to organizations situated abroad;

d) *Depreciation*: Depreciation must normally be based on the rates fixed by the tax department.

The annual rates (on the straight line method) currently accepted can be summarised as follows:

	% Per Annum
Furniture and decorations	10
Office equipment and calculating machines	15
Electrical equipment	10
Airconditioners	25
Desert coolers	20
Motor cars and trucks	25
Motor vans	15
Buildings	3
Buildings and road construction equipment	12½
Survey equipment	10
Tents	20
Pumps	20
Small Tools	20
Aircraft	15
Ships	5
Launches	20
Large drilling equipment	7½

Depreciation must be adjusted to the lower of book and the rates accepted by the tax department. The accepted rates vary from time to time and may be negotiated with the department if circumstances (for example multishaft working) can be shown to justify this.

A depreciation schedule for all fixed assets must be submitted as part of the tax return.

e) *Losses*: These cannot be carried back or forward; it is, accordingly, most important to avoid losses in the first years of a commercial or contracting business giving rise to increased profits in later years.

f) *Bad Debts* may be deducted only when legal action is shown to have been taken against the defaulting debtor.

g) *Pre-operational Costs*: Pre-operational costs not attributable to capital expenditure may normally be written off over the lesser of three years or the life of the project. In the case of banks, all such expenses must be written off in the first accounting period.

E. Payments to Non-Residents

The tax department seeks to tax all payments made to non-residents for services rendered or used in Saudi Arabia and will assess a taxpayer as agent for the non-resident. This covers payments to sub-contractors for services, plant hire rentals, etc., and also insurance premiums and bank interest paid to a non-resident company and banks. Substantial arbitrary assessments of the profit element on these payments may be made by the tax authorities. It is understood that the tax department at present imputes a profit element of at least 15% to relevant payments for insurance, rental payments and bank interest.

The tax applied to imputed profits is calculated in the same manner and at the same rates as set out above. The tax due is payable on the company tax due date and is subject to the normal penalties for delay.

The company's auditors must certify all amounts paid to and names and addresses of relevant non-residents.

F. Corporate Entities Available and Other Structures Available

The basic company law is set out in the regulations for companies which was published by Royal Decree in 1965 as amplified by subsequent administrative resolutions.

Apart from Sole Proprietorships, there are basically seven distinct types of corporate organisations capable of being organised under Saudi Arabian commercial law; there are:

— Joint Liability Partnership,
— Mixed Liability Partnership,
— Mixed Liability Partnership by Shares,
— Limited Liability Partnership,
— Company with Variable Capital,
— Joint Stock Company,
— Cooperative Company.

Each is briefly considered below.

Joint Liability Partnership

This is an association of two or more partners who are jointly and severally liable for the debts of the partnership to the extent of their entire personal or corporate assets.

Mixed Liability Partnership

This consists of two categories of partners, at least one of which must be a general partner who is liable for the debts of the partnership to the extent of his entire assets, and the other category including at least one limited partner who is liable for the debts of the partnership only to the extent of his own contribution to the capital thereof.

Mixed Liability Partnership by Shares

This is a partnership consisting of two groups: one group comprising at least one general partner who shall be liable for the debts of the partnership to the extent of his entire assets, and another group comprising at least four share partners who are liable for the debts of the partnership to the extent of their capital shares only and whose capital is not less than SR 100,000. The capital is divided into negotiable indivisible shares of equal value and the value of each share must be not less than SR 50.

Limited Liability Partnership

From a practical point of view, the so-called Limited Liability Partnership (LLP) is normally chosen by foreign investors.

The basic reason for this is the complexities involved in forming a joint stock company as this requires a Royal Decree, which is normally only given for major projects.

The LLP is very similar in form to a French SARL. The basic characteristics and requirements are as follows:

— A LLP is a 'partnership' consisting of two or more partners. All partners have limited liability. The number of partners is limited to 50.
— The minimum capital requirement is SR 50,000 paid up in full at subscription.
— A LLP may not seek public subscriptions in raising or increasing its capital.
— A LLP must appoint auditors who are duly licenced to operate in the Kingdom.
— Shares shall confer equal rights to the net profits and in the partners equity upon liquidation, unless the memoranda of association provides otherwise. Every partner shall have the right to participate in deliberations and in voting, and shall be entitled to a number of votes equal to the number of shares he owns. However it is permissible to agree otherwise.
— 10% of the net profits must be set aside annually as legal reserve. The partners may decide to discontinue the deduction when the reserve totals half the capital.

Variable Capital Partnership

This is defined as a partnership whose by-laws provide that its capital may be increased by new payments from the original partners or by admission of new partners and whose capital can also be reduced by the partners by reduction of their capital.

Joint Stock Company

The capital of a Joint Stock Company shall be divided into negotiable shares of equal value and the shareholders shall be liable only to the extent of the value of their shares. In such companies, the number of members shall not be less than five.

The capital of a Joint Stock Company which offers its shares to the public for subscription shall not be less than SR 1,000,000. In other cases the capital of the company shall not be less than SR 200,000, made up of shares with an individual value not less than SR 50.

A joint Stock Company can only be incorporated by Royal Decree and a company so registered shall be deemed to have Saudi nationality but this shall not necessarily debar it from rights as may be granted to non-Saudis.

Co-operative Company

A Joint Stock Company or a Limited Liability Company may be founded on a co-operative basis for the benefit of all partners and through their joint efforts if it aims at:

— reducing the cost price, purchase price or sale price of certain products or services, or
— improving the quality of the products or the standards of the services which the company supplies to the partners or consumers.

The capital of the Co-operative Company shall be divided into registered shares which shall be of equal value. The value of each share shall not be less than SR 10 or more than SR 50 but each of the shareholders in a Co-operative Company shall have equal rights.

Other Structures Available

A foreign company can also operate in the Kingdom under the following structures:

— branch,
— Joint-Venture,
— representative office under the sponsorship of a registered Saudi business entity.

Each structure is examined briefly below.

Branch: It is possible to register a branch of a foreign company in Saudi Arabia. In the longer term however it might be necessary to have a full Saudi partner. Therefore it may be cheaper to bring him in 'ab initio' rather than be subjected to pressure later on.

Branches of foreign corporations are taxed at the same rates as corporations.

Branches are generally used to carry out a specific Tax exempt government contract. In that case the activity will by definition be tax free in the Kingdom.

Joint-Venture: In a joint venture one of the forms of partnership is used with the joint venturer who must a Saudi national and will in this case also act as sponsor; profits, losses and finance are shared in the proportions agreed by the venturers. The foreign interest in the venture must be registered and it will be taxed as if it were a foreign branch, or company.

Representative Office: The representative activity is generally handled on a 'sponsorship' basis. In this case, the supplying companies should preserve the position of doing business 'with the Kingdom' rather than 'in the Kingdom'. If such is the case there will be no Saudi taxation as the representative office will have no Saudi income.

G. Formation Procedures

Foreign investors must obtain an initial authorisation for the type of activity they wish to commence, from the Foreign Investment Office.

Requirements necessary are as follows:

- Copy of the Memorandum of Association of the foreign company,
- Copy of the company's Board of Directors Resolution approving the opening of an office or a branch duly authenticated,
- Activities to be performed by the company inside the Kingdom,
- Projects carried out by the company outside the Kingdom,
- List of officers reponsible for the project in the Kingdom,
- Capital allocated for the project,
- List and value of the equipment and machinery owned by the company.

In addition, all commercial and industrial establishments must register within one month of commencement of business with the local registration offices of the Ministry of Commerce and Industry. Additional units or branches must also be registered.

Further to both of the above, general information relating to the proposed business must also be provided to the Ministry of Labour and Social Affairs before operations are commenced, and registration must be effected at the office of the General Organisation for Social Insurance.

Detailed model of internal regulations for companies is set out in

Resolution 583 of 1385 of the Council of Ministers. Variances from this format must be approved by the Ministry of Commerce and Industry.

H. Incentive Legislation

a) Incentives are available to foreign investors under the Foreign Capital Investment Code[3] subject to a minimum Saudi participation of 25% and approval of the project by the Minister of Commerce and Industry, a tax holiday of five years from the commencement of production will be granted to investors in 'economic development projects'. Economic Development Projects are not defined in the code, but may, as a generalisation, be taken as meaning investment in industrial manufacturing. In some circumstances, it may be possible for contractors to obtain this status but it appears that the Saudi Authorities are now understood to be insisting on at least 50% Saudi participation if tax and other privileges are to be granted.

b) In addition, foreign investors in approved projects may obtain the privileges extended to Saudi nationals under the Statute for Encouragement and Protection of National Industries. These can include:

1) Exemption from customs duties on imports of machinery, tools, spares, raw material and packaging,
2) Provision of factory sites at nominal rents,
3) Customs tariff protection,
4) Financial assistance.

I. Taxation Treaties

No bilateral treaty for the avoidance of double taxation has been signed.

J. Foreign Exchange and Money Control

There are no foreign exchange regulations in Saudi Arabia nor limitations on dividends, loans, repatriation or introduction of funds. All necessary movements of finance can therefore be carried out without permission being required. A minor exception is the compulsory deposit of the investment in share capital which must be maintained in a separate bank account during registration procedures.

3. Law 35 for 1964.

Chapter IV
Sudan

Companies

A. Basic Principles

An entity is regarded as resident in the Sudan if control and management of the affairs of such entity is exercised in the Sudan in the year of assessment.

Entities thus defined as resident, including companies, trustees, partnerships and other corporate or unincorporated bodies of persons, are assessable to tax on their world wide income.

B. Tax Rates

Tax rates vary according to the nature and residence of the taxable entity. Current rates are as follows:

a) Sole traders and partnerships,
b) Private limited companies,
c) Public limited companies,
d) Non resident companies.

The rates currently in force for each category (before surcharge) are:

Taxable Profit in US $			*Rates of tax in %*			
			Category			
			(a)	(b)	(c)	(d)
0	to	436	–	25	25	25
437	to	769	5	25	25	25
770	to	1,282	15	25	25	25
1,283	to	2,564	20	25	25	25
2,565	to	10,256	30	40	40	40
10,257	to	25,641	40	40	40	40
25,642	to	51,282	50	50	45	50
51,283	to	76,923	50	60	50	50
76,924	to	102,564	60	60	50	60
102,565	to	128,205	60	60	50	60
Over 128,205			All categories 60.			

From 1976 a development tax surcharge amounting to 5% of the tax liability is charged to all businesses earning a profit of more than £S 1,000.

The liability for Business Profits Tax is due in two equal instalments as follows:

	Financial year ending	
	before June	*after June*
1st Instalment	31st October	30th April
2nd Instalment	30th April	31st October

C. Other Taxes

Capital gains

A capital gain tax of 40% is charged on any capital gain resulting from the sale of land or buildings in towns as well as agricultural land in the province of Khartoum or any other province to be decided by the Minister of Finance, Planning and National Economy.

D. Computation of Taxable Income

Taxable profits and losses are based on the trading results shown by the financial accounts adjusted for tax purposes. The following are amongst the matters for which adjustments may be required:

a) Remuneration of each part-time director is limited to the greater of 15% of taxable profits or £S 2,000, but restricted in total to 30% of assessable profits.

b) Interest paid is deductible only if:
— subject to tax on income in the hands of the recipient person,
— paid to a bank,
— paid in respect of a loan received outside Sudan and used in earning income subject to business profits tax.

c) Bad debts may only be deducted if proven unrecoverable.

d) Final and pre-operating expenses may be charged against profits in equal instalments over 10 years; any excess charge will be disallowed.

e) Depreciation at the following annual rates computed on cost:

Buildings	2 1/2%
Plant & Machinery	7 1/2% - 15%
Motor Vehicles	20% - 25%
Furniture	7 1/2%

f) Losses may be carried forward against profits for five years; the right to do so is lost if audited accounts are not submitted in any one year.

g) Where two or more businesses are held as to more than 10% by any one person, he will be assessed to business profits tax on the aggregate of his shares of profit or losses of all relevant businesses.

E. Corporate Entities Available

Foreign Interests may participate in the share capital of Sudanese Companies provided the appropriate official consents are obtained; permission will not normally be given for non-Sudanese capital to control Sudanese companies.

G. Incentive Legislation

The policy is set out in:
- the Development and Promotion of Industrial Investment Act of 1972,
- the Development and Promotion of Investment in Economic Services Act of 1973,
- the Development and Promotion of Agricultural Investment Act of 1976.

All three are discretionary acts and enable the Minister of Industry and Mining, the Minister of Finance and Commerce and the Minister of Agriculture Food and Natural Resources to grant a number of concessions to approved projects.

These can include:
- Corporate tax exemptions for three to six years,
- This period might be extended if the capital return over the first period was less than 10%,
- Exemption from custom duties,
- Industrial land at concessionary prices,
- Reduction in the rates of facilities (electricity, freight, etc.).

The Acts further give guarantees in respect of:
- Transfer of profits outside Sudan,
- Capital repatriation in the same currency in which it was imported — this includes original capital imported plus profits capitalised,
- Non-discrimination between national, foreign, public or private sector enterprises,
- Guarantees against nationalisation and confiscation.

H. Taxation Treaties

The only country with which Sudan has signed at present a double taxation agreement is the United Kingdom (ratification is awaited).

Relevant features are as follows:

— Profits of an enterprise of a contracting state shall be taxable only in that state unless the enterprise carries on business in the other contracting state through a permanent establisment situated therein. A permanent establishment includes a building site or construction or assembly project which exists for more than twelve months.

— The treaty rejects the principle of force of attraction of a permanent establishment.

— No profits shall be attributed to a permanent establishment by reason of the mere purchase by that permanent establishment of goods or merchandise for the enterprise.

— Dividends: The tax treaty allows a 15% withholding tax on the gross amount of the dividends distributed by a company in one state to a company in the other contracting state.

— If a company in one state owns 10% or more of the shares of a company in the other state, no tax is due in the contracting state of which the company paying the dividends is a resident.

I. Foreign Exchange and Money Control

a) Capital repatriation

Capital invested in a project can be repatriated in the currency in which it was originally brought into the country, provided it was registered with the exchange control.

b) Remittance of profits, dividends and interest

This is permissible, but the approval will be given in the same currency as that in which the relevant capital was imported.

c) Exchange rates

The conversion has to be done at the official rate of exchange. There is a surcharge of 15% for foreign exchange leaving the country and a discount of 15% for money brought into the country.

Chapter V
The Gulf States in Summary

A. Introduction

In a number of the Gulf States tax decrees have been issued in the Fifties and Sixties but generally an unusual position arises in that it is not the practice of the fiscal authorities concerned to collect tax to which it is clear they are entitled by law. In other cases no tax decrees have yet been issued. Therefore it seems appropriate to divide the different states into three groups; the states applying the tax decree, the states where the tax decree is not currently of general application, and the States without tax legislation.

B. List of States

States without Tax Legislation of General Application

Bahrain
Fujeirah

States where the Tax Decree is not currently of general application

Abu Dhabi
Ajman
Dubai
Ras Al-Khaimah
Sharjah
Umm Al-Qawain

States where Tax Decrees are of general application

Oman (to non-nationals)
Qatar (to non-nationals participating in shareholding companies)
Kuwait (to non-nationals)

C. Kuwait Income Tax Decree and Company Structure

The different decrees issued have all been modelled on the first Kuwait income tax decree issued in 1951 which was amended in 1955 and 1957. It is therefore useful to analyse briefly the tax position in Kuwait. It should be stressed however that differences exist between the various Income Tax Decrees and that reference should be made to them in specific cases.

a) Main Provisions

When originally enacted the Kuwait Income Tax Decree was intended to apply only to foreign companies[1] which at the time were oil companies.

The amendments of article 2 (f) of the Decree in 1957 and the company law make bring within the scope of the tax *all* bodies corporate (both Kuwait and foreign) carrying a business in Kuwait: 'The term body corporate, wheresoever incorporated carrying on trade or business in Kuwait includes any body corporate carrying on trade or business in Kuwait either directly or through an agent and also any body corporate carrying on trade or business in Kuwait as an agent for others.'

Until recently it has not been the general practice of the Taxation Authorities to make assessment on companies other than oil companies but recently the authorities have sought tax returns from two classes of body corporate operating in Kuwait:

— Foreign Contractors,
— Companies or Partnerships in which foreign bodies corporate have registered interests.

Tax legislation is enacted in such a way to exclude partnerships: '*no individual* who is a member of a partnership whether such partnership includes a body corporate or not *shall be subject to Kuwait Income Tax under the existing Income Tax Decree*'.

But any body corporate which is a member of a partnership carrying on trade or business in Kuwait is subject to Kuwait Income Tax on the amount of its share of the partnership profits.

The term carrying on trade or business in Kuwait is defined to exclude trading requiring no other work or service inside Kuwait.

Oil companies are subject to special regulations which are not covered in this study.

1. Article (2) F Tax decree 1955, Explanatory Notes: The tax was to be imposed on every body corporate but since there was no law in Kuwait which provided for the formation and registration of such associations, the term 'Body Corporate' could be applied only to companies or other associations registered abroad.

b) Computation of Trading Income

Taxable profits are based on accounts prepared on normal commercial principles. Depreciation is deductible at the following rates:

	%
Buildings	4
Office furniture and equipment	15
Motor car and motor cycles	33 1/2
Lorries and trailers	25
Marine Craft	7 1/2.
Construction equipment	25
Other plant and machinery	10

Losses can be carried forward without limit.

c) Structures Available

Joint Venture Branch: All foreign branch activity in the State must be carried out through a Joint Venture with a Kuwaiti who is a licensed commercial agent and has at least 51% participation in the profits of the venture. It has no legal existence except as between the parties and is not binding on third parties. It merely provides a form by which joint venturers may formalise their arrangements inter se.

A Limited Liability Partnership (WLL).

This is an association of not more than 30 Natural persons (individuals can act as nominees for foreign companies).

Each person is liable only to the extent of his share in the capital.

Its members shall not be less than two in number.

A Limited Liability partnership constituted in Kuwait shall be of Kuwait nationality, at least one of the partnership members shall be Kuwaiti and its registered office shall be in Kuwait.

The share of the Kuwaiti members must not be less than 51% of the total company's shares.

The minimum capital is KD 7,500 ($26,000) to be fully paid upon subscription.

The shares of the company are registered and are freely transferable between members, but side letters with the other partners are commonly obtained to protect the foreign partner.

There is a pre-emptive right of purchase of an outgoing partner's share available for the other partners. This is limited to a first option to purchase at a price no less than that offered by third parties.

A WLL may not engage in insurance, commercial banking or investment on behalf of third parties.

Kuwait Closed Share Capital Company (KSC Closed):

The company has a separate legal existence and the liability of each subscriber for the company's obligations is limited to the nominal value of his shares.

The registered office shall be in Kuwait.

The Kuwaiti capital must aggregate at least 51% and admission of any foreign capital is subject to Government consent.

The shareholders can either be natural persons or legal entities.

The minimum capital requirement is KD 7,500 ($26,000) of which 20% should be paid in upon subscription. The balance to be fully paid after 5 years from the date of the company's decree of incorporation.

In the event public subscription is sought at a later date, the minimum capital becomes KD 37,500 (US $130,000).

Foreigners may be directors but a majority of the directors must have Kuwaiti nationality.

At least 10% of the gross profit must be set aside each year as legal reserve. There reserves may not be distributed to the shareholders.

No person may be on the board of directors of more than *three* Kuwaiti shareholding companies.

A general shareholder's meeting must be held annually to approve the Board's report and the balance sheet, appoint auditors and approve the distribution of the dividends.

The accounts must be kept according to Kuwait Law and must be certified by auditors registered in Kuwait.

D. Comparative Rates

A comparison of the rates stipulated by the various Decrees in terms of US Dollars in set out in the following table:

COMPARATIVE TAX RATES

	Kuwait	Qatar	Abu Dubai	Dubai	Oman
Highest rate	55%	50%	50%	50%	50%
Adjusted Profits in US $ m	over 1.3	over 1.27	over 1.28	over 1.28	over 1.08
Lowest rate	5%	5%	10%	10%	5%
Adjusted Profits in US $ m	over 0.018	over 0.018	over 0.26	over 0.26	over 0.016
Scale	marginal	marginal	slab	marginal	marginal

E. The Other States

a) Bahrain

Subject to the requirement that foreign participation may not exceed 49% foreign investors in Bahrain can generally choose whichever form of business enterprise best suits them. Foreign companies are permitted to register branches in Bahrain provided 51% National control is retained.

To operate in Bahrain the foreign investor will need a license. The application for the license will be made by the sponsor.

Corporate entities available are basically the same as in Kuwait although there are differences in detail. For the foreign investor the choice will be between a shareholding company or a limited liability partnership or a joint-venture branch without legal status.

No general tax decree has been issued in Bahrain and as a result there are no taxes on income, sales, capital gains nor on earnings, salaries, dividends or interest.

b) Oman

Under the foreign business and investment law, no foreigner may engage in business activity or invest in Oman except through an Omani commercial company formed under the Commercial Companies Law. National interests must have at least a 35% participation. The minimum capital requirements for a company with foreign participation is OR. 150,000. Certain types of activity require a higher Omani interest than 35%; these are:

Press and Publicity	66%
Public Utility	51%
Real Estate	51%
Shipping or Aircraft	51%

Development projects or specifically exempted companies can have a 100% foreign interest; this is the case for:

- Companies, institutions and individuals which are engaged in activities in the Sultanate of Oman by virtue of agreements or special contracts concluded with the government of the Sultanate or its public institutions;
- Companies, institutions and individuals which are engaged in a project declared to be an Economic Development Project;
- Companies, institutions and individuals who are engaged in a profession which the Council of Ministers has declared to be a profession of critical need and shortage in the Sultanate of Oman;
- Companies and institutions which are licensed banking institutions in the jurisdiction of their organisation; and

— Companies, institutions and individuals which are exempted by Sultani Decree.

Forms of business legal entities: Here again the practical choice for the foreign investor will be a limited liability partnership. It is also possible to set up a joint stock company. Both are juristic persons. Some foreign companies are doing business in Oman under the form of a joint-venture. A joint-venture is not a legally incorporated body.

Capital structure, paid in capital at subscription, formation procedures, liquidation procedures etc., vary slightly in detail from Kuwaiti Company Law.

Foreign companies are permitted to register fully owned branches in Oman.[2] For tax purposes they are considered to be companies. However the business of Commercial Agency can only be engaged in by Omani's or 51% Omani owned companies.

Tax System: The income tax decree dates from 1971. Income tax is imposed on every body corporate wheresoever incorporated carrying on trade or business in the Sultanate of Oman through a permanent establishment.

If the Sultan considers that for the general betterment of the economy of the Sultanate the provisions of the Decree should not be applied to a specific body corporate or group of bodies corporate, he may exempt the body or bodies for such a period he deems appropriate.[3]

c) Qatar

The commercial legislation requires a minimum Qatari participation of 51% in any business venture (branch or company) with a proportional number of Qataris on the board.

Non Qatari persons, natural or juristic may by decree be exempted from the 51% local participation requirement if the project is accepted as 'economic development project'.

No person, real or juristic shall be allowed to engage in commerce or open a commercial or industrial establishment in Qatar without registering in the commercial register and without obtaining a licence from the Commercial Registry. Registration shall be renewed every 5 years.

Agencies may only be held by Qatar nationals or 100% Qatari owned companies.

No foreign contracting company shall have permission to practice business in Qatar, unless it appoints a service agent whose nationality is Qatari. The functions of the service agent shall be confined to facilitating relations between the company and the authorities.

2. Branches established in Oman of foreign companies are exempt from the provisions of the foreign business and investment law requiring the formation of an Omani Company with Omani participation.

3. Article 1 of the Income Tax Decree.

'Works Contracting Firms' must have 100% Qatari capital, but the legislation permits exemption in cases where foreign investment is deemed to be in the national interest.

Forms of business legal entities: The commercial legislation provides for the formation of shareholding companies which can expressly be exempted from income tax if they are accepted as development projects.

Foreign participation in commercial ventures is normally carried out either:
— By joint venture branch,
— By minority participation in a Qatari company.

The first alternative is often chosen as the formation of a Qatari company is time-consuming and involves an Amiri Decree; accordingly foreign investors for non-industrial projects in Qatar often choose a joint venture association under the sponsorship of a Qatari trader.

Tax Systems: The income tax decree is based on the Kuwait Decree. Legislation exists for the taxation of all bodies corporate, but it has not been the general practice of the Taxation Authorities to made assessments on companies other than oil and foreign participation in Qatar companies not exempted by virtue of the Industrial Development Law. No tax appears to be levied at present on joint venture branches, but there is no guarantee that this situation will persist in the future.

d) United Arab Emirates

Although each Emirate regulates commercial activity in accordance with the Decrees of its Ruler, it is the intention of the Federal Government to seek uniformity of commercial legislation over a period of time.

In order to appreciate the salient differences between the territories comprising the UAE, there is set out a brief description of the current fiscal and registration position in each. In all Emirates, it is necessary to obtain a trade licence (which expires after one year, renewable within one month of the date of expiration) to carry on commercial activity and in most cases a foreign trader will be required to obtain a bank guarantee for DH 100,000 (US $25,600).

Abu Dhabi: In any business enterprise of whatever nature there must be a local partner or a National sponsor and agent. Incorporated entities normally require the participation of Abu Dhabi capital to the extent of at least 51% in the capital of a company particularly where the company is seeking to benefit from government incentives.

A national sponsor is required by all contractors and his remuneration is limited by a sliding scale of 1% to 2% depending on the size of the contract.

A taxation decree of general application is in force, but in practice, tax has to date only normally been levied on oil companies or the branches of foreign banks; fees are charged for the trade licence which is calculated on a flat rate scale dependent on the trade involved.

Dubai: The percentage of Dubai capital required in a Dubai incorporated company is considered on a case by case basis by the Government department concerned and some National capital is normally required; it is however still possible (after obtaining the appropriate municipal consents) to register the Dubai branch of a foreign (i.e. non UAE) company with totally foreign capital. In the absence of a sponsor, the foreign investor must offer a bank guarantee valid for a period of 15 months of DH 100,000 at any local bank.

Dubai has a general tax decree, but has only used it for oil companies; foreign banks are taxed at rates stipulated by their charters.

Formal tax exemptions are available by Amiri Decree.

In the absence of taxation on income, annual fees are levied. These are as follows:

10% of rent paid on office premises,
5% of rent paid by all partners for their residential accommodation plus DH 300 for the licence itself.

In the investors countries these fees do not normally qualify as credits against domestic taxes as they are not considered to be of a comparable nature to taxes on profits.

Sharjah: The position is generally similar to Dubai in that no regulations have been made in Sharjah as to the maximum percentage of foreign capital permitted in a Sharjah registered company; As yet there are no laws governing minimum number of directors, shareholders or auditors, no specified legal reserve, no rules on liquidation. However legislation facilitating the establishment of companies will be enacted in the future. As a result Sharjah has been extensively used as the situs of holding companies formed by non-Sharjah Arab groups for offshore activity.

It is also still relatively easy to obtain permission for a foreign (i.e. non UAE) company's branch to carry out a commercial activity in Sharjah.

There is an income tax decree of general application but so far no tax on corporations has been levied, (other than on oil companies). However it is understood that a low tax of some 1% on both corporate and personal income of Sharjah residents is now under consideration.

As in Dubai, annual fees are chargeable, the amounts of which are:
20% of rent of business premises
10% of rent of residential premises.

The Other Emirates:

Ajman	Umm Al-Qawain
Ras Al-Khaimah	Fujeirah

The above have relatively few commercial entities and fewer locally incorporated companies; the latter have been incorporated on a case-by-case basis, normally for a specific and limited local purpose.

There are no laws governing sponsorship, minimum number of directors, auditors, company by-laws, capital requirements, legal reserve.

Both Ajman and Ras Al-Khaimah are potential locations for holding companies, as no local capital requirements have been established and a few have been incorporated.

In Ajman, Ras Al-Khaimah, Umm Al-Qawain tax decrees of general application have been issued, but it has not been the historic practice of the taxation authorities to make assessments on companies. No tax decree was issued in Fujeirah. There is no guarantee however that such taxfree situation in the Emirates will continue in the future.

As in Dubai and Sharjah annual fees are levied. These are:

15% of the amount of rent paid for business premises, plus
7% of the rent of domestic premises.

Problems are not normally encountered in registering branches of foreign (i.e. non UAE) companies.

e) Summary of Minimum Local Capital Requirements

Abu Dhabi	: 51%
Ajman	: No local capital requirements
Bahrain	: 51%
Dubai	: Ruler's discretion
Fujeirah	: No local capital requirements
Kuwait	: 51%
Oman	: 35%
Qatar	: 51%
Ras Al-Khaimah	: No local capital requirements
Sharjah	: No local capital requirements
Umm Al-Qawain	: No local capital requirements

F. Incentive Legislation

a) Abu Dhabi[3]

Any industrial company which satisfies certain conditions, can be granted exemption from income tax on profits for the first five years of operation, and from income tax on reserve funds set aside from the projects after the five-year period, if these reserve funds are used for improvement or expansion purposes and provided that they do not amount to more than 50% of the total annual profits.

3. Abu Dhabi Law of Industry for 1967.

Sites may also be assigned to the company free of rent for five years.

In any case, Abu Dhabian participation in the capital of the project must not be less than 51%.

b) Kuwait[4]

Subject to the administrative discretion of the Ministry of Commerce and Industry exemptions can include:

- Loans to manufacturing businesses which are available through the Industrial Bank of Kuwait at a low interest rate, currently 4%;
- The Kuwait Municipality may provide free land to approved manufacturing businesses in certain specified industrial areas;
- The Ministry of Commerce and Industry is empowered to grant tax holidays at their discretion of up to 10 years.

There is however no exemption available from the agency or Kuwaiti participation laws which restrict the importation of goods to Kuwait is and require 51% Kuwaiti participation in companies formed under Kuwaiti law or branches registered as doing business in Kuwait.

c) Oman

Tax exemptions are available to:

- wholly Omani companies for a period of five years up to 11 June 1980,
- for five years from establishment for industrial, agricultural or fishing companies,
- for up to five years (with possible extension for further five years) for 'companies with a paid up capital of more than Riyals 100,000 and contributing to the economic development of the Sultanate'.

d) Qatar

The net annual profits realised by Qatari share companies may be exempted from taxes for a period of 5 years, on condition that their purpose shall be to establish and operate a project necessary for the development of the country.

The exemption is restricted to national shareholding companies and exclude foreign branches and individuals.

4. Kuwait Industry Act.

Territory	Law	Nr. and Year Issued
Bahrain	Commercial Companies Law	No. 28 of 1975
Egypt	The Companies Law	No. 26 for 1954
	Consolidated Taxation Laws	No. 14 of 1939 and No. 99 of 1947
	Commercial Business Licenses	Ordinance 32/69 for 1969
	Development and Free Zone Law	No. 43 for 1974
	Model Development Statutes	No. 92 for 1975
Iraq	The Companies Law	No. 31 for 1957
	Income Tax Law	No. 95 for 1959
	Major Development Project Law	No. 157 for 1973
Kuwait	Income Tax Decree	No. 3 for 1955
	Commercial Company Law	No. 15 for 1960
	Law of Commerce	No. 2 of 1961
	Industry Act	No. 6 for 1965
Oman	Income Tax Decree	1971
	Commercial Company Law	1974
	Commercial Agencies Law	No. 26 of 1977
Qatar	Income Tax Decree (as amended)	No. 1 for 1954
	Share Company Law	No. 3 of 1961
Saudi Arabia	Income Tax Regulations (Basic Decree)	
	Foreign Capital Investment Code	No. 35 for 1964
	The Company Decree	M 6 for 1965
Sudan	The Companies Ordinance	1925
	Sudan Business Profits Tax Ordinance	1967
	The Development and Promotion of Industrial Investment	1972
	The Development and Promotion of Investment in Economic Services Act	1973
	The Development and Promotion of Agricultural Investment Act	1976
United Arab Emirates	Abu-Dhabi Income Tax Decree	1971
	Dubai Income Tax Decree	1969
	Sharjah Income Tax Decree	1969

Part III
The Investors' Systems

Introduction

The purpose of this part is to summarize the background that the investing company needs to bear in mind when it is contemplating the structure of Middle East operations.

The chapters on each jurisdiction follow a common basic pattern and in addition introduce special features where these are likely to be of particular significance.

The pattern is:

— Basic principles of taxing foreign income,
— Tax rates applicable to foreign source income,
— Double taxation relief provisions (very few treaties are applicable),
— Branches abroad,
— Participations in foreign entities,
— Withholding tax.

Additional sections have been added in relation to particular countries wherever this seems justified; examples being:

— for the United States, DISC and other special provisions of the 1976 tax reform act;
— for West Germany, the incidence of anti-avoidance measures (Aussensteuergesetz) and the special provisions applicable to developing countries;
— for France, the exceptions to the principle of territoriality in relation to initial investment costs and a short introduction to the avoir fiscal and précompte system;
— Perhaps the most controversial issue that is of major significance at this time is the provision of the 1976 US tax reform act that determine the applicability of foreign tax credit by reference (inter alia) to the compliance or otherwise of the US corporation with the Arab League Boycott.

Chapter I
Belgium

Corporation Income Tax

A. Basic Principles

A resident corporation is subject to taxation in Belgium on its worldwide income.

A resident corporation is defined[1] as

— a corporate entity, (i.e. having legal personality)
— pursuing profit or involved in profitable operations,
— having in Belgium either its registered office or its principal place of management and control.

A company registered abroad can also be regarded as a resident in Belgium if it is managed and controlled in Belgium.[2]

Partnerships are treated as companies where they have a legal entity separate from their members. However in prescribed circumstances election may be made for taxation on the level of the individual members rather than on a corporate level.

B. Tax Rates

Resident companies in Belgium are chargeable to corporate income tax at the flat rate of 48% on their worldwide taxable income.

However, companies in which individuals hold not less than 50% of the shares and which do not fall to be regarded as holding companies are chargeable at reduced rates on taxable income not exceeding BF 15 million.[3]

1. Article 94 Code des Impôts sur le revenu (hereinafter CIR).
2. Article 102 CIR.
3. Article 126 CIR.

C. Double Taxation Relief Provisions

The foreign income of a resident company is subject to corporate tax together with the Belgian income. To reduce the tax burden of the foreign income being already taxed abroad a number of bilateral double taxation treaties have been signed but none was concluded with Egypt, Iraq, Saudi Arabia, Sudan or the Gulf States. In the absence of treaties the law foresees the following unilateral relief provisions:[4]

- Profits earned through a permanent establishment abroad as well as income from foreign real property are taxed at one quarter of the corporate tax (unless of course the income is exempt by Treaty). This results into an effective rate of tax of 12%.
- Personal property income including royalties and dividends from 'non-permanent' investments in foreign entities (as defined below) which are taxed abroad, are granted a flat foreign tax credit equal to 15% on the net amount received.
- Dividends from 'permanent' investments in foreign entities are exempt from Belgian taxation to the extent of 90% or 95% depending upon whether the Belgian company qualifies as a holding company or not.

Foreign income taken into consideration is always the net amount received after deduction of the foreign income or withholding tax with the exception however of the dividend income from 'permanent' investments in foreign entities which is to be reported at 105% of the net amount received.

D. Branches Abroad

General rule

In a treaty situation the profit of a permanent establishment is taxable only in the country where it is situated.

As no treaties yet have been signed with a Middle East country, the statute law is applicable. As stated above, the statute law provides a unilateral relief measure resulting in the taxation of foreign branch income at an effective tax rate of 12%.

For the relief provision to apply, it is required however that the profits are both *realized* and *taxed* abroad.

Realized abroad: Profits of a foreign branch are by definition considered to be realised abroad[5] but the Code does not give any clear definition of a 'foreign branch'. The Code only stipulates that profits will not be

4. Articles 111, 128, 187 CIR.
5. Commentaries IR (hereinafter Comm. IR) 88/8.

considered as realized abroad if the profits result from operations which are managed from the Belgian company, as the place from where all instructions are given and where all the results finally converge without the intervention of agents or a permanent establishment abroad.[6]

Taxed abroad: Income is considered taxed abroad if the income has been subject to the tax regime applicable in the foreign country. Therefore no relevance is attached to:
— the form of tax applicable abroad (e.g. schedular or global tax, taxation on a real or notional basis),
— the fact that some elements of the foreign income are not taxed abroad as a result of the internal legislation (e.g. certain special concessions and allowances granted) even if this is in contradiction with the Belgian rules.[7]

Basis of taxation

For tax purposes, the foreign establishment is first considered as a separate economic entity having its own profits and expenses. Both these two components of the taxable income of the foreign branch will be determined according to *Belgian* statute law. This necessitates adjustments to the taxable income as determined by the foreign country in order to arrive at taxable income in accordance with Belgian tax principles.

Transfer of merchandise from the Belgian Head Office to its foreign branch has to be priced at arms length basis.

Operating expenses have to be recorded separately by each establishment and are only deductible from the corresponding income e.g. interest payments made by the Head Office to third parties in respect of the branch abroad are to be charged to the branch and are not deductible from Head Office income.

Common expenses, duly justified, are to be allocated proportionally between Head Office and foreign branch:[8] general and administrative expenses paid by the Head Office for the overall worldwide business are to be attributed accordingly.

Trading losses: The losses of an establishment located in a country with which Belgium has not signed a Tax Treaty are to be deducted[9]
— first from the profits of establishments subject to the reduced rate,

6. Comm. IR 88/10.
7. Comm. IR 88/11.
8. Comm. IR 43/7.
9. Comm. IR 110/13.

— next from the profits of establishments located in countries with a convention,
— finally from profits realized in Belgium.

The balance of trading losses may be carried forward and set off against taxable income from the succeeding five years or for an unlimited period in the case of initial losses incurred during their first five financial periods by companies incorporated during certain defined periods. Loss carry-back is not allowed.

E. Participation in Foreign Entities

The Income tax code recognises the principle of 'permanent investments'. Dividends received from a permanent investment qualify for a dividend income deduction.

Broadly the following are defined as *'permanent investments'*:[10]

— Shares which have been held by a corporation during the whole of the financial period in which it has received the related dividends;
— Shares which are redeemed or exchanged as a result of a merger, split or reorganisation of a corporation, provided the corporation holding such shares, has held them since the beginning of its financial period during which the shares were redeemed or exchanged;
— Shares received which were obtained as a result of a merger, split or reorganisation of a corporation, provided the corporation, holding such shares, has held them until the end of the financial period during which the shares were exchanged.

The percentage holding in a qualifying corporation is not relevant.

Basis of charge for dividends of permanent investments: Dividend income from permanent investments in foreign entities is to be reported as taxable income by the receiving corporation at 105/100 of the net dividend received (that is after deduction of the foreign withholding tax). The mark up of 5% relates to a fictitious dividend tax which is granted to the receiving corporation. The mark up will be credited against the corporate income tax payable by the receiving corporation and any excess credit is refundable.

The dividend income deduction is equal to 95% or 90% in the case of an holding company as defined in the fiscal code.[11] The deduction will be computed on the net dividends received [illegible]ding the mark up.

10. Article 112 CIR.
11. Article 113 CIR (paragraph 2).

Example

Belgian corporations receiving foreign dividends from 'Permanent investments'.

Belgian corporation (not a holding) receives:

		Cash
Net dividend after foreign withholding tax	100.00	100.00
Fictitious foreign with tax 5% on 100.00	5.00	
Sub total	105.00	
95% deduction on 105.00	(99.75)	
Subject to corporate tax	5.25	
Corporate tax: 48% on 5.25	2.52	
Credit for fictitious foreign with tax (5% on 100.00)[12]	(5.00)	
Excess refunded	(2.48)	2.48
Cash received		102.48

Belgian holding company receives:

		Cash
Net dividend after foreign withholding tax	100.00	100.00
Fictitious foreign with tax 5% on 100.00	5.00	
Sub total	105.00	
90% deduction on 105.00	(94.50)	
Subject to corporate tax	10.50	
Corporate tax: 48% on 10.50	5.04	
Credit for fictitious foreign withholding tax (5% on 100.00)[13]	(5.00)	
Excess due	0.04	(0.04)
		99.96

Basis of charge for dividends of non-permanent investments: In this case the dividend income deduction is not available but instead a tax credit is granted in order to avoid the double taxation of the income. The foreign tax credit is equal to 15% of the net amount received that is after deduction of the foreign withholding tax.

The credit is given only if the foreign source dividends have been subject to a foreign income tax.

Example

Foreign dividends from 'non permanent' investments:

12. Refunded if exceeding fiscal liability.
13. Refunded if exceeding fiscal liability.

Belgian corporation (not a holding) receives:

		Cash
Net dividend, after foreign withholding tax	100.00	100.00
Corporate tax: 48% on 100.00	48.00	
Foreign tax credit: 15% on 100.00[14]	(15.00)	
Corporate tax payable	33.00	(33.00)
Cash received		67.00

F. Foreign Interest or Patent Royalties

The exemption received for dividends does not apply, nor do the relief provisions provided for in article 128. Double taxation is in this case only partly prevented by a lumpsum tax credit.

Foreign interests or patent royalties are subject to the company income tax for their net amount received i.e. less expenses, foreign withholding and income taxes. Against the corporation tax, the company is allowed a fixed credit equal to 15% of the net amount received. This credit is only granted if the income has been subject to a foreign income tax, regardless of the actual amount of foreign tax withheld or assessed. The income received is not grossed up by this fixed credit.

14. Not refundable.

Chapter II
France

Corporation Income Tax

A. Basic Principles

Tax is chargeable on profits realised by enterprises operating in France, and on profits attributed to France by an international agreement.[1]

This means that:

— the criteria for liability to taxation adopted for corporations by the French system is the source of income, residence is not relevant;

— a French company will not suffer French tax on profits realised abroad:

  — either by a company or through a permanent establishment,

  — or even in the absence of any entity or representative when the operations realised abroad constitute a complete commercial cycle. The expression 'complete commercial cycle' has not been as such defined in the 'Code Général des Impôts', case law must therefore be considered in order to form an opinion. Basically, however, it means all the simultaneous or successive commercial and civil operations needed to realise a profit;

  (*Example*: a complete commercial cycle is formed in France when a foreign company buys and sells goods in France without bringing any alteration to it.)

  (*Note*: It is not essential that the commercial cycle takes place in a single country and that the income is taxed abroad.)

— tax is chargeable in France on the foreign source income of a French company which doesn't originate from:

  — one of its companies or permanent establishments abroad,

  — the accomplishment of a complete commercial cycle.

1. Article 209-1 Code Général des impôts hereinafter CGI).

B. Tax Rates

Companies resident in France are subject to corporate tax on their income derived from or related to business activities carried on in or from, France at a rate of 50%. There is a 50% tax on short term capital gains and 15% on long term capital gains.

C. Double Taxation Relief Provisions

France has signed a number of treaties for the avoidance of double taxation but no treaty was signed with one of the countries of our study.

In all other cases of this study the tax law in the investors' countries provides in the absence of treaties for unilateral relief measures. In the case of France there is no system of unilateral foreign tax relief. Any foreign tax paid on income arising in a non treaty country would be deductible as an expense from taxable income only and no tax credit is available.

D. Branches Abroad

The fiscal law[2] applies the principle of territoriality of income as opposed to that of residence. The courts have used two criteria to determine when profits are to be regarded as arising from a French source:
— whether a permanent establishment (ètablissement stable) exists, or
— accomplishment of operations forming a *complete commercial cycle* even in the absence of a permanent establishment.

Permanent establishment

Three factors determine the existence of a permanent establishment:
— There must be a permanent place of business;
— The activity of the establishment must contribute to an increase in value of the goods or service from which the company hopes to profit (plant, building site, but not just stocking);
— The establishment must stand by itself as a separate commercial entity, for example it must have its own customers independent from the head office.

If a branch exists abroad:
— Profits of the foreign branch are not chargeable to French tax;
— On the other hand, charges related to these operations are not deductible from taxable profit in France;

2. Article 209-1 CGI.

— Losses realised abroad cannot be set off against profits in France.

But problems do arise in determining whether a branch exits or not. In accordance with article 209 of CGI corporation income tax is chargeable on profits realised by enterprises operating in France and on profits attributed to France by an international agreement.

Recently a court decision shed some more light on the interpretation of the concept of territoriality.[3] A French company signed a contract to deliver in Roumania a complete factory for the production of X, the French company being responsible for the erection and initial operation, and the supply of technical expertise and training of personnel. At the completion of the contract the French company declared as taxable income half of the profits of the deal.

The court ruled that *in the absence of a bilateral treaty* (which was the case) these should be considered as profits realised by the company operating in France and thus liable to corporate income tax, profits from operations realised abroad but connected with other operations of the company and at the same time not constituting a separate commercial entity. (See definition of a permanent establishment page 103.) This is effectively the case in a contract where a company agrees to a global price:
— to deliver abroad a complete factory ready to start operation;
— to supply the necessary staff for the training of the local personnel and the operation in the early production stage,
— and when all the pre-studies are conducted in France and the personnel is executing purely technical work, they are not acting as representatives of the company abroad, even though remuneration is to be paid by the foreign customer.

It was concluded that in the absence of a separate commercial activity exercised abroad all the profits from such a contract are subject to tax in France. Therefore French investors entering into contracts in one of the countries of this study should be aware that no bilateral treaties have been signed with any of these countries. Careful consideration should therefore be given in drafting the contracts in order to avoid the possibility of double taxation.

In some cases the solution will be to make several contracts in order to avoid paying taxes on all the profits, (supply contract and erection contract) in other cases it might be possible to operate through a foreign branch or if it is suitable the answer might be to create a foreign subsidiary.

Complete commercial cycle

As mentioned before[4] French companies are exempted from corpora-

3. No. 11/75-INF 1126 (BIC-111, 30 bis) (TA, Paris 13 Mars 1975 No. 2344/3033/1971).
4. See page 102.

tion income tax in France on profits realised from operations performed abroad which constitute a complete commercial cycle.

E. Exceptions to the Principle of Territorality[5]

Exceptions to the principle of territorality are as follows:

— Two provisions are to be considered in respect of French investment abroad:

a) The Old Provisions[6] continue to apply to establishments and offices which were created before April 1, 1973. Under these provisions enterprises holding investments abroad may deduct certain expenses relating to these investments from their taxable income in *France.* The relevant expenses are:

- market research expenses incurred with a view to establishing a sales office, a research office or an information office abroad,
- expenses including overheads, depreciation, financing costs, taxes, provisions, etc., borne in the operation of the establishment or office for the first three tax years of its existence.

These deductions may be 'temporary' or 'final'. Temporary deductions apply to agencies or branches but not to subsidiaries. They only result in a cash flow advantage for the enterprises benefiting from them. Amounts deducted must subsequently be included in taxable income in equal instalments in the five tax years following the three tax years mentioned above. Final deductions may be granted only by the Ministry of Finance.

b) The New Provisions[7] make a distinction between commercial enterprises and industrial enterprises; the deduction remains temporary in both cases:

Commercial Enterprises: The enterprises can obtain relief from tax for losses borne during the first five years of operation of their foreign establishment, up to a limit of capital invested in the establishment during this period. Amounts deducted must however be carried forward and added to taxable profits in five equal instalments starting with the sixth year.

For certain countries on a list drawn up by the Ministry of Finance, a deduction may be claimed equivalent to total capital invested in the establishment in the first five years of the operation abroad. Amounts deducted must be carried forward and added to the taxable profits in five equal instalments starting with the sixth year.

5. Article 39 Octies CGI.
6. Article 39 Octies 1, 2, 3 CGI.
7. Article 39 Octies A 1, 2, 3, 4 CGI.

Industrial Enterprises: The deduction is allowed only with the approval of the Ministry of Finance on the advice of the Ministry of Industrial and Scientific Development. Qualifying enterprises may establish a provision free of tax for a sum equal to a fraction of the amounts invested in capital during the course of the first five years of operation of the establishment. This fraction cannot exceed one-third of the sums invested.

Another exception envisaged by the CGI is the consolidation of worldwide profits.[8] Although provision is made for it, only a few companies in France have acquired such status.

French companies which have received the approval of the Ministry of Finance to consolidate, may include profits and losses of all branches and subsidiaries located in France and abroad in their taxable base. This constitutes a double exception to the general rules:

Contrary to the principle of territoriality under the worldwide income concept, the profits of permanent establishments located abroad and operations constituting a complete commercial cycle outside France are included in the taxable base in France.

The principle of consolidation of profits which globalises all profits as earned by a simple entity is totally foreign to the basic concepts.

F. Participations in Foreign Entities[9]

French resident companies holding at least 10% of, or which own shares whose cost was at least FF 10 million in another French or foreign company, are granted special benefits relating to the taxation of the dividend income from qualifying holdings.

In effect, the parent company (Maison mère) suffers nominal or nil tax on dividends received from its subsidiary. It includes in its profits only 5% of the gross dividends (before withholding tax) received from a foreign subsidiary regarded as the share of expenses and charges incurred during the course of the taxable year. If for example, a foreign subsidiary distributes a dividend of 100, the parent company would be taxed as follows. In this example it is assumed that there was no withholding tax and thus the gross and net dividends are the same.

Dividend from the subsidiary (Gross Dividend)		100
Deductions	0	
Net Dividend	100	
Share of expenses (5% of gross dividend)	5	(95)
Taxable base		5

8. Article 209 quinquies CGI.
9. Article 145-146-216 CGI.

This 'reintegration' is not the equivalent of taxation on dividends, but an adjustment of the charges paid by the parent company. In effect[10] the portion reintegrated may not exceed the total expenses of the parent company. Thus if the latter has no expenses, the taxation would be:

Income from the subsidiary		100
Deductions		
Income from the subsidiary	100	
Share of expenses	0	(100)
Taxable base		0

The 5% taxable portion is thus the amount added to taxable income on which French corporation tax at the rate of 50% is applied resulting in a tax of 2,25% in the case of a dividend received from a *foreign company.*

If the French resident company holds less than 10% in the foreign company taxes imposed by the country of source on the recipient company will be deductible in computing taxable income. The foreign tax deductible is the tax on dividends not the underlying tax on profits.

G. Avoir Fiscal and Précompte

As mentioned above, when certain conditions are met, the parent company does not pay any tax on dividends which it receives from its subsidiary.

When the parent company re-distributes to its own shareholders dividends received from a French or foreign subsidiary, it is subject to the 50% précompte on the net amount distributed.

Where the dividend received by the parent company is from a French subsidiary, the précompte is off-set by the avoir fiscal of 50% of net dividends which may be credited against the précompte. However, this avoir fiscal is not granted with respect to dividends received from a foreign subsidiary.

H. Taxation of Foreign Interest, Patent Royalties

Although the French company income tax is in general based on the territoriality principle, by exception foreign interest and patent royalties may be subject to the French company income tax. Taxes imposed by the country of source on the recipient company are considered as deductible expenses in computing taxable income.

If however, patent royalties and interest are earned through a permanent establishment in the foreign country, they will generally be exempt in France.

10. Article 211-2 CGI.

As mentioned above, the recipient company may elect to be subjected to the company income tax with respect to worldwide income and in this case gross foreign source patent royalties and interest income will be included in taxable income. Any foreign income or withholding tax will be credited against the French company income tax.

I. Anti Avoidance Measures

Consent from the Investment Control Department is required for any direct investment abroad including the acquisition of a controlling interest in a foreign company, if it exceeds one million Francs in any one year or relates to holding, investment, portfolio, financing or financial companies.

Therefore no intermediate company can be formed without first obtaining government consent.

Subject to the provisions against non arm's length transactions[11], sales of assets by French companies to a foreign company are not controlled, whereas contributions to the capital of a foreign company as mentioned above may require Government consent.

11. Article 57 CGI.

Chapter III
West Germany

Corporation Income Tax

A. Basic Principles

Resident corporate entities are subject to unlimited tax liability to West German taxation on income from all sources, both domestic and foreign. German corporate income tax law distinguishes between taxpayers subject to unlimited and limited tax liability, residents have unlimited liability and non-residents limited liability; Resident companies are those whose seat or place of management is in West Germany.

B. Tax Rates

Corporation Tax (Körperschaftsteuer)

The new reform applied as of January 1st, 1977 contained changes in tax rates and the national affiliation privilege ceased to be applicable without resulting in any disadvantages.

The general rate for resident companies is *56% on undistributed profits.* Distributed profits are taxed at a rate of 36%.

In addition to the corporate income tax, companies are subject to the following *direct tax.*

Therefore if the income was previously subject to tax at the rate of 56% the tax burden is reduced from 56% to 36%.

If, on the otherhand, tax exempt income (for example, intercompany dividends qualifying for the affiliation privilege) is distributed, the rate is increased from 0% to 36%.

As a result all distributed profits of a corporation subject to unlimited tax liability are subject to corporation tax at the rate of 36%. The system adopted is similar to the French 'avoir fiscal and précompte' and the equivalent of the 36% corporation tax is available as a credit against the personal income tax liability of a resident recipient of the dividends. Non-residents are not entitled to claim a credit for the corporation tax.

Example 1: Undistributed profits

Profit before income taxes	100.0
Trade tax on income assuming it is 20% (20% of 83.3)	(16.7)
Sub total	83.3
Corporation tax 56% of 83.3	(46.6)
Profit after income taxes	36.7
Total German Income Tax burden	63.3

Example 2: Distributed Profits to Shareholders

Profit before income tax	120
Trade tax on income approx. 20% of 100	(20)
	100
Corporation tax 36%	(36)
Gross dividend	64
Capital yields tax 25% of 64	(16)
Net dividend	48
Shareholder's taxable income 48+16+36	100
Personal income tax 30% (assumed) of 100	30
Tax credit for the resident shareholder (16+36)	52
Personal income tax	(30)
Amount refundable to shareholder	22

If the income of a corporation is distributed to resident individuals, the corporate tax is totally eliminated and the total income suffered at the level of both the corporation and the individual shareholder will depend on the personal income tax rate of the individual receiving the dividend. It should be mentioned though that the corporation income also triggers the trade tax on income as explained below.

Trade Tax on Income (Gewerbeertragsteuer)

The exact burden varies from community to community but is normally in the range of 15 to 20% of taxable income as computed for corporate income tax purposes. Trade income tax is a deductible expense for corporation tax purposes.

C. Double Taxation Relief Provisions

Foreign tax suffered on income earned in non treaty countries may be credited against the German corporation income tax imposed on the same income for the same period. However, the nature of the foreign income tax must be equivalent to German income or corporation tax.

If the foreign tax is not considered equivalent to German income or corporation tax, it may not be credited but may be treated as a deductible expense.

In no case can the foreign tax credit exceed the amount of the equivalent German corporation or income tax attributable to the foreign income.

Certain provisions contained in the Income Tax Ordinance[1] restrict credits for foreign income taxes paid against German income tax liability, for example:

— Only foreign national income taxes are available for credit. State, provincial and local income tax are thus ineligible for foreign tax credit but may be deducted as expenses.
— Foreign income taxes available for credit only are limited to German income tax on the same income; any excess foreign tax credit is lost.
— Only specific types of income[2] qualify for credit of foreign tax suffered thereon, e.g. export sales to a non-resident buyer do not qualify as foreign source of income. Therefore, if a foreign income tax is levied on direct sales by a German enterprise, such tax is neither credited nor deductible.

D. Branches Abroad

a) Statute Law

Under the 'worldwide income' concept, a German resident company with branches in a non Treaty country is subject to corporation tax (not the trade tax) on income or profits of those branches, irrespective of whether those profits have been remitted to Germany.

If the foreign branch is liable to taxes abroad, the foreign tax may be credited against German income tax.[3]

Foreign taxes qualifying for credit are creditable against corporation tax on the same income for the same period.

b) Basis of Charge

The profit of a foreing branch may be computed under either the *direct or indirect method.* According to the direct method the branch is treated as if it were an independent business firm. In practice, this method can be applied only if separate books are maintained and separate financial statements are prepared for the branch. Under the indirect method, the profit of the branch is computed as a part of the profit of the entire

1. Article 68 (a) Income Tax Ordinance.
2. Article 68 (b) Income Tax Ordinance.
3. See Double Taxation Relief Provisions page 110

enterprise through allocation proportionally to key factors e.g. turnover, number of employees, assets, etc.

The direct method is generally preferred and even required by a number of tax treaties.

Certain charges by the head office to the branch are not permitted as deductible expenses; for example, royalties for patents owned by the enterprise, rental charges for equipment owned by the head office and made available to the branch, interest on 'loans' by the head office. Interest payments by the head office to third parties for financing the branch abroad are generally allocable.

Losses of foreign branches are deductible in Germany.

The arm's length principle is to be applied to income of German enterprises derived from business dealings with related foreign companies.[4]

c) Treaty Situation

Applying the OECD model, it is usually agreed that the profits of the foreign branch (permanent establishment) are taxed in the foreign country.

The branch is considered in the foreign country as a separate entity of the company as a whole and the taxable profits are those attributable to the permanent establishment if it were an independent enterprise engaged in the same activity under the same conditions and dealing at arm's length with the enterprise of which it is a permanent establishment.

Interests on loans, royalties and rental charges from the head office to the branch are normally not deductible from the profits of the foreign branch. However, in the computation of its profits, allowable deductions are all expenses wherever incurred, which are reasonably connected with the profits so taxable including executive and general administrative expenses.

Sales of goods from the head office to the branch have to be carried out at arm's length principles.

If according to a tax treaty the income of a foreign branch is exempt from German taxation, a loss of such a branch is not normally deductible in Germany. However[5], a loss sustained by a branch located in a foreign country can — to the extent such loss exceeds any tax-exempt income from other branches in that country — be deducted from the taxable income of the German head office, even if this deduction results in a loss at the level of the German taxpayer. If in subsequent years a branch in this foreign country realizes taxable profit, it has to be added back to the taxable income of the German taxpayer to the extent of the branch's losses deducted from the German source income, unless the German taxpayer

4. Aussensteuergesetz.
5. Article 2 Foreign Investment Act.

can prove that according to the law of that specific country a loss sustained by a branch cannot be deducted from income of another assessment period.

E. PARTICIPATIONS IN FOREIGN ENTITIES — AFFILIATION PRIVILEGE

a) Old Provisions: If a resident company owns 25% or more of the shares of another resident company and provided this ownership exists for at least 12 months prior to the end of the taxable year in which the profit distribution is received, the distribution of dividends to the first company by the latter is tax exempted. The exemption applies both to *capital yield tax* which would otherwise have to be withheld by the paying company *to corporate income tax* (which would have to be paid by the recipient) to the extent that the recipient entity re-distributes the dividends to its shareholders and trade tax on income.

b) New Provisions: With the new corporate tax reform, the affiliation privilege applicable to intercompany dividends becomes superfluous for corporation tax purposes. Indeed a domestic corporation will likewise individuals have the benefit of the deductibility of the 36% corporation tax paid by the distributing corporation. The affiliation privilege will continue to apply for the trade tax, net worth tax and double taxation treaties.

c) If a domestic corporation receives a dividend from a foreign subsidiary which would be non taxable under the 'affiliation privilege' under the old tax provisions had it been received from a domestic subsidiary, the domestic corporation may claim an indirect foreign tax credit for the proportionate share of taxes paid by the foreign subsidiary on the income out of which the dividend was paid. As one of the requirements the foreign subsidiary must have no or almost no passive income. Such indirect foreign tax credit may also be claimed for taxes paid by second-tier foreign subsidiary. This is to the extent its dividends to the first tier foreign subsidiary have been redistributed to the German corporation.

The dividends received must be grossed up by the amount of indirect foreign tax credit claimable.

If the share in the foreign participation is less than 25% no credit for indirect taxes is granted.

d) If the qualifying foreign subsidiary is located in a developing country the indirect foreign tax credit is deemed equal to the German corporation income tax on the dividend from such subsidiary so that no tax becomes due on such dividends in Germany. Dividends from subsidiaries located in Iraq, Egypt, Saudi Arabia, Sudan and the Gulf States could therefore become tax exempted in Germany from corporate tax and trade tax on income.

e) The affiliation privilege applies by extension (in amended form) to trade tax and net worth tax.

f) Foreign Subsidiary Losses: If the parent company holds at least 50% of the shares of the foreign entity or 25% of the shares if the subsidiary is situated in a developing country, the parent company may set up a tax free reserve in respect of the subsidiary's losses in the year of investment and the following four years, but this must be added back to income to the extent profits are generated but not later than in the 5th year. The amount of the reserve is limited to the value of investment.

F. Withholding Tax

Profit distributions are subject to the normal capital yields tax according to national law which is regularly 25%. The withholding of its capital yields tax, which is a tax liability of the recipient of the dividend, may be waived under certain conditions when distributions are made to tax payers with unlimited tax liability. Taxpayers with limited tax liability are under certain circumstances entitled to file, in accordance with tax treaty regulations, an application with the German Federal Fiscal Office for partial refund of the 25% capital yields tax withheld.

G. Anti Avoidance Measures in Germany[6]

If resident individuals or corporate shareholders together hold more than 50% of a non-resident intermediate company's capital or more than 50% of its voting rights, the income of the subsidiary is attributed on a percentage basis to the German shareholders provided the income of the intermediate company is deemed to be passive and subject to foreign income taxes not exceeding 30%.

The German law defines those types of income that do not constitute intermediate company income. Basically the provisions apply to income from intermediate companies which result from non-productive activities.

H. Developing Countries Tax Law

A major benefit of the Developing States tax law is the classification of certain foreign States as:

— Developing, or
— Least Developed.

6. Section 7-14 Aussensteuergesetz.

Deductible reserves of respectively 40% and 100% are permitted in respect of investments in Developing and least Developed States.

The Middle East States principally considered in this study are classified as follows:

Developing	*Least Developed*
Bahrain	Sudan
Iraq	
Egypt	
Kuwait	
Oman	
Qatar	
Saudi Arabia	
United Arab Emirates	

Accordingly a German company with a subsidiary or branch in Sudan, would be entitled to deduct from taxable income the total foreign investment. The reserve must be set aside in the fiscal year during which the investment was made.

A German company with a subsidiary or branch in Egypt, Iraq, Bahrain, Kuwait, Oman, Qatar, Saudi Arabia or UAE would be entitled to deduct from taxable income 40% of the total foreign investment.

In both cases the amounts deducted must be reintegrated into taxable income at a minimum annual amount of 16.67% beginning with the sixth business year following the one in which the reserve was formed. In some cases the reserve may be released by means of annual credits to income of not less than 8.33% of the reserve beginning with the sixth business year following the one in which the reserve was formed.

The portion can change from year to year; however, as mentioned above, they must amount to at least 1/6 or 1/12 respectively. Theoretically the reserve could be released to income in one year.

A requirement for the above reserves is that the subsidiaries or branches in developing countries are engaged exclusively or mainly in the following activities:

— The production and sale of merchandise (except weapons),
— The extraction of natural resources,
— Agriculture and forestry.

The grant of the above tax concessions cannot be applied if it creates a loss in the parent company.

I. Foreign or Interest Patent Royalties

Interest and patent royalties received from abroad are included in the taxable income but a credit is granted for foreign income taxes paid.

Chapter IV
Japan

Corporation Income Tax

A. Basic Principles

Domestic corporations are liable to corporate income taxes on their entire income. Subject to the corporation tax are not only corporation in the ordinary sense but also all other juridical persons and certain organisations without juridical personality.

B. Tax Rates

Japanese corporate income taxes consist of *corporation tax* (National Tax) and local taxes which are *business tax, prefectural inhabitant tax and municipal inhabitant tax.* The rates vary depending on the corporation's paid in capital and the amount of taxable income. The effective corporate income tax rate could be as high as 54%.

C. Double Taxation Relief Provisions

Domestic corporations can claim a credit for foreign taxes applicable to corporation tax and inhabitant tax but not business tax.

1) Ordinary Foreign Tax Credit

Foreign corporation tax (including foreign local tax) is creditable against the Japanese corporation tax for the taxable year in which the foreign tax accrues, subject to the following overall limitation:

$$\text{Japanese Corporation Tax} \times \frac{\text{Total income from sources outside Japan}}{\text{Entire income subject to Japanese corporation tax}}$$

In computing total income from sources outside Japan, a net loss incurred in any foreign country may not be taken into account at the corporation's option. The entire income subject to Japanese corporation tax is the amount before the deduction of the losses carried over from previous taxable years.

If the foreign taxes accrued in any taxable year exceed the limitation computed for that year, the excess may be carried over for the five succeeding taxable years or carried back to the five preceding taxable years.

Foreign corporation tax incurred may, at the corporation's option be deducted from taxable income as necessary expenses. If a domestic corporation elects to take foreign taxes as a credit, such foreign corporation taxes may not be deducted. The corporation must exercise its choice on the total amount of foreign taxes accrued in each taxable year.

D. Branches Abroad

a) Statute Law

A domestic corporation with branches overseas is subject to Japanese taxes on profits of those branches, irrespective of whether those profits have been remitted to Japan.

If the income has been subject to foreign corporation tax (including any foreign local tax and withholding tax) credit is available against Japanese corporation tax and inhabitant tax but not against business tax.

As a domestic corporation is subject to Japanese corporation and inhabitant taxes on its overall profits, losses of a foreign branch are set off against Japanese profits.

b) Treaty Situation

Japan has concluded a bilateral tax treaty for the avoidance of double taxation with Egypt (convention of August 1969 with respect to taxes on income).

If a Japanese enterprise has a permanent establishment in Egypt, such permanent establishment shall be considered to have distributed as dividends in Egypt within 60 days from the closing of its financial year, an amount equivalent to 90 per cent of its total new profits liable to tax on industrial and commercial profits: such dividends shall be deducted from the amount of taxable income or profits subject to the tax chargeable in respect of its industrial and commercial profits and shall be subject only to the tax on income derived from movable capital, the defence tax, the national security tax and the supplementary tax.

The remaining 10% is only subject to the tax on commercial and industrial profits but is set aside to form a special reserve.[1]

1. Article 8.3 of Bilateral treaty for the avoidance of double taxation signed between Japan and Egypt.

Note

The term 'permanent establishment' includes a building site or construction or assembly project which exists for more than *six months.*

E. Participations in Foreign Entities

Indirect foreign tax credit is given if a domestic corporation receives dividends from foreign corporations (hereinafter referred to as 'foreign subsidiary') meeting the following conditions:

a) Not less than 25% of shares issued, or of paid-in capital of foreign subsidiary or not less than 25% of shares with voting powers of the foreign subsidiary are owned by the domestic corporation for at least six months.
b) The foreign subsidiary is a corporation established for the purpose of carrying on business in that foreign country and is not established for any tax consideration.

Any foreign corporation tax imposed on the profits of the foreign subsidiary which are to be distributed as dividends to the domestic parent corporation is creditable against the Japanese tax of such domestic corporation.

The foreign corporation tax which is applicable to the dividends is computed as follows:

$$A \times \frac{\text{dividends received}}{B - A}$$

where

A is foreign corporation tax imposed on the foreign subsidiary,
B is income of the foreign subsidiary.

Income of the foreign subsidiary used as 'B' above is whichever larger of the following:

a) Income of the foreign subsidiary on the basis of which dividends to be distributed are computed, or
b) Income computed according to the foreign laws on corporation tax provided that the corporation tax treated as an expense and income exempt from the corporation tax are also included.

It should be stressed that if a Japanese company owns less than 25% in a foreign company, no indirect foreign tax credit is allowable. A credit for the foreign withholding tax paid on the dividend will be granted.

F. Tax Free Reserves and Other Special Deductions

Reserve for Overseas Market Development

Provisions for the cost of overseas market development may be deducted as expenses, if a corporation with capital of not more than 1,000 million yen derives income wholly or partly from 'overseas transactions'.

The main activities of 'overseas transactions' are as follows:

- Export of goods or sale of goods to an exporter,
- Processing of goods by the order of an exporter,
- Large-scale repairing of ships paid, directly or indirectly, in foreign currencies.

There is a maximum amount deductible depending on the corporation capital.

One-fifth of the amount credited to the reserve in one accounting period shall be added back successively to the income in five succeeding years.

Reserve for Overseas Investment Loss

If a corporation acquires the shares of the companies mentioned below which are issued for the creation or the increase of capital of such companies (including dividends or distributions from companies) or extends credit to the following companies under specified conditions in the form of loans or purchase of debentures and credits a certain amount of the acquisition and other costs to the reserve account in order to meet possible losses of the value by the decline in their prices, etc. such amount is deductible as expense to the extent that the amount does not exceed 50% and in some cases 100% of such acquisition costs. The amount credited to the reserve may be held for five years, but from the sixth year one-fifth of such amount shall be added back to the income in five succeeding years.

- Specified overseas business company: defined as an 'overseas business company' which has its main office in a developing country (i.e. all the Middle East States of our Study): 30% reserve. However, a holding company or a company established abroad mainly for tax considerations is excluded.
- Natural resources development company: 40% reserve.

Overseas Technical Service Transactions

If a corporation has derived income wholly or partly from 'overseas transactions of technical services', a special deduction from taxable income is allowed.

This includes the following:

- Patent, know-how, etc. resulting from the research work in the corporation concerned, which is alienated or offered in exchange,

directly or indirectly, for foreign currency or its equivalent;
- Copyrights (except the right to screen the cinematograph films) sold or offered in exchange, directly of indirectly, for foreign currency or its equivalent.
- Such technical services as planning, consultation, supervision, etc. related to the construction or production of plant or equipment, or specified technical services for agriculture or fishery, and surveying performed in exchange for foreign currency or its equivalent, on condition that the compensation for such services is 2 million yen or more per contract.

The amount deductible is 55% in the case of patents etc. and 20% in all other cases. The deduction, however, shall not exceed 50% of the total ordinary income.

Expenditures in Prospecting for Mineral Deposits or Overseas Mineral Deposits

Prospecting for mineral deposits or overseas mineral deposits is encouraged by the following special exemption system:
- The amount credited to the overseas prospecting costs reserve by a domestic mining corporation may be deducted as an expense. The amount deductible shall not exceed 50% of income (before corporation tax) derived with respect of the minerals received from foreign corporations satisfying certain conditions.
- The amount thus reserved shall be added back to the income after three years. If the corporation having the prospecting costs reserve uses the reserve for prospecting costs, the tax deferment is then converted into an exemption from taxable income.

There is no exemption from Japanese corporation tax for dividends paid out of profits exempted abroad by reason of industrial incentive.

G. Tax Evasion Measures

An important provision in the Japanese tax law against the use of tax havens by companies stipulates that an overseas affiliate or a subsidiary should be one which is established for the purpose of conducting business in the foreign country concerned rather than purely for tax considerations.

Chapter V
Netherlands

Corporation Income Tax

A. Basic Principles

Under Dutch tax law, profits are defined as all benefits, whatever their source or nature, accruing to a taxpayer. Worldwide profits of a resident company are therefore subject to tax. Capital gains are treated as normal business income. Companies are subject to corporate income tax as residents, if:

— they are incorporated under the Dutch law, or
— they are 'actually situated' in the Netherlands — the most important factor in the determination of where a company is actually situated is the location of the company's central management.

B. Tax Rates

Corporate income tax is the only tax on profits of companies with capital wholly or partly divided into shares. It is not a schedular tax, but unitary and all income from whatever source is therefore combined to form worldwide income.

The tax rates are as follows:

	D Fl	%
Up to	40,000	45
Amount between	40,001 - 50,000	60
Over	50,000 total income subject to	48

C. Double Taxation Relief Provisions

As mentioned, a Dutch resident corporation is subject to tax on its worldwide income. Unilateral relief is however available under the following conditions:

— *No Treaties or other measures are applicable.*

— *The income must be subject to income tax in the relevant foreign country:* The basic principle is that the unilateral tax relief is granted if the foreign income has been taxed abroad; 'taxed' means that profits of the foreign branch *in principle* be liable to foreign tax on its *profits of a nature similar to Dutch income tax.*[1]

Whether or not any foreign tax is actually paid is immaterial nor is the rate of tax relevant. For example should the foreign company pay no foreign tax or be liable to a reduced rate of tax by virtue of statutory investment incentives in the foreign country relief will still be applicable.

In contrast to some tax legislation, the Dutch system does not look at the effective amount of foreign tax paid. Thus if the foreign tax suffered is less than Dutch corporation tax on the equivalent income, there are some global tax savings. To the extent that the rate of foreign tax is higher than the Dutch tax rate, there is however no relief for the excess tax.

– *The income must be considered as foreign source income.*[2] Basically foreign source income is composed of:

a) Profits derived through a *permanent establishment* as defined in the Decree[3] or a permanent representative situated outside the Netherlands:

A permanent establishment means a fixed establishment of an enterprise through which the enterprise's activities are wholly or partly carried on, including the seat of the management of the enterprise, and agricultural land as well as works the execution of which takes more than twelve months.

The following is not considered to be a permanent representative:

i) an entirely independent representative;
ii) a representative who has no authority to conclude transactions, even though he may hold a stock for urgent deliveries.

A permanent establishment or a permanent representative shall be deemed not to exist where goods are held only on a commission basis;

b) Foreign net income other than profits from a foreign enterprise arising from:

— personal services related to an employment performed abroad,
— immovable property situated abroad,
— debt claims on immovable property located abroad secured by mortgage,
— foreign participation rights under certain circumstances,
— rights to periodical payments and public welfare benefits at the expense of a foreign public body.

1. See F. J. Fesevur, Vaste inrichting en 'gelijksoortige' belasting, Weekblad voor fiscaal recht No. 5203 of November 21, 1974.

2. Article 2 Unilaterai Decree for the Avoidance of Double Taxation.

3. Article 2.4 Unilateral Decree for the Avoidance of Double Taxation.

If the above three conditions are met, proportional relief is available.

In principle, two main methods of computing foreign tax credits are recognised under the unilateral relief measures. These are the exemption and the credit against tax methods.

The Exemption method, in principle, exempts foreign source income according to the following formula:

$$\text{Amount of tax reduction} = \frac{\text{foreign income}}{\text{total taxable income}} \times \text{Dutch tax on total foreign and local income}$$

e.g.	Foreign income	100
	Foreign tax 40%	(40)
	Net foreign income	60
	Local income	100
	Foreign income (grossed up)	100
	Total income worldwide	200
	Dutch tax at 48%	96
	Amount of relief 100/200×96 =	48

Therefore for a company, the unilateral relief provisions can provide a total exemption of foreign source income.

The Credit method allows a credit against the Dutch income tax for the lower of the foreign tax actually levied or the amount computed on the basis of the above formula. One of the drawbacks of the credit method is that if the total income of the recipient of the foreign source income is nil or negative, the amount of credit is lost. The Royal Decree of June 4, 1976 terminated this situation. The Decree provides that if the amounts of credit in any year cannot be used against the income tax due over that year, the excess can be carried forward and offset against the tax liability over any of the following six years. This method only applies to dividends, interest and royalties, not qualifying as income from immovable property secured by mortgage, and received from a less developed country.

D. Branches Abroad

Statute Law

Dutch resident companies operating through one or more branch offices in non treaty countries may be eligible for relief from double taxation according to the Dutch Unilateral Decree for the Avoidance of Double Taxation.[4]

4. See Double Taxation Relief Provisions, page 121.

The basic conditions that must be fulfilled if profits are to be exempted from corporate income tax in Holland are:
- The existence of a bona-fide permanent establishment in the foreign country,
- The branch income must have been subject to a tax comparable with Dutch tax on income.

Basis of Charge

Profit is calculated in Dutch currency in accordance 'with sound business principles'. The method used in measuring the income attributable to a permanent establishment is always the direct method. Therefore, the resident taxpayer and the permanent establishment are treated as completely separate entities and separate accounting records must be maintained. As relations between head office and branches can complicated and not clearly defined, uncertainties and discussions with the tax inspector are often encountered.
- Each establishment must maintain a separate record of its operating expenses and these are deductible only from the corresponding income.
- Sales of merchandise between the branch and the head office must be priced on an arm's length basis.
- Common expenses duly justified are to be shared accordingly.
- Losses made by a foreign branch are compensated with the profit of the resident Dutch company in the year in which the losses occur. Relief from double taxation is only applicable when profits exceed losses compensated in the past.

E. Participations in Foreign Entities

1. Dividends received by a Dutch company from foreign participations are exempted from Dutch tax if the following basic conditions are met:[5]
- The Dutch recipient company must hold at least 5% of the equity share capital of a foreign corporation;
- The foreign company must have been subject to a tax comparable with Dutch tax on income (in determining comparability withholding taxes on dividends are ignored);
- The Dutch company must hold the participation from the beginning of (the Dutch company's) fiscal year in which a distribution is made;
- The participation must be held for a business related purpose and not for investment purposes;

5. Article 13 Corporation Tax Law; the exemption is referred to in Dutch as 'deelnemingsvrijstelling', usually translated as 'affiliation privilege', or 'participation exemption'.

— The distributing entity must be a non-resident company and not an investment trust.

2. *Capital gains* arising on sales of shares regarded as a qualifying investment are equally exempted from Dutch tax.

Costs (e.g. research costs, financing costs) incurred in connection with the acquisition of a substantial participation in a resident company are deductible from the taxable income of the purchaser, but this is not extended to similar costs relating to foreign participations. This means that interest on loans to acquire a foreign participation is not deductible.

As dividends from qualifying foreign participations are exempt no tax credit can be claimed for foreign withholding taxes on these dividends. The foreign withholding tax on such dividends is not admitted as a deductible expense.

F. Scope of the Netherlands Tax Exemption for Holding Companies

The scope of application of the exemption was the subject of a court decision in 1973.[6]

The Case

On November 7, 1973, the Dutch Supreme Court held that a Dutch company holding the shares of two German companies did not qualify for the dividends received exemption with respect to dividends distributed by these German companies since the Dutch company was deemed to hold the shares of the German companies as a passive investment. The Supreme Court held that a corporate shareholder not carrying on any business activities of its own must be considered to own a passive investment, because there does not exist a relationship between its business (there being none) and the business of the distributing companies. The Supreme Court deemed the participation to be a portfolio investment and not an asset held for business related purposes.

The tax authorities later issued a document clarifying their position. This ruling can be summarised as follows:

— For shareholdings of a Dutch Company in foreign companies, the dividends received exemption will be available if the Dutch company holding the shares has a basic function ('wezenlijke functie') for the business operations of the group of companies to which it belongs, either at the top of the concern structure or somewhere in between.

— The dividends received exemption does not apply to participations in a

6. Decision of Hoge Raad November 7, 1973, No. 17.182, BNB 1974/2.

non resident company which directly or indirectly acts as a company holding passive investments such as non resident investment holding companies. It was however, specifically confirmed that a Dutch intermediate holding company which is used as a 'link' between the business activities of a non-Netherlands parent company and non-Netherlands subsidiaries will qualify for the participation exemption. A 'link' includes a company which is used for purposes of channeling dividends and collecting capital gains for a group. An intermediate holding company of this type does not hold shares in subsidiaries by way of passive investment. In the case of a Netherlands top holding company, not only the nature of the subsidiaries but also the function of the holding company is relevant in determining the availability of the participation exemption. A top holding company which is used for example, for purposes of policy making, management, or finance will benefit from the participation exemption for all subsidiaries except subsidiaries which are used as an investment company.[7]

G. Use of the Dutch Affiliation Privilege by Foreign Corporations

The treatment afforded to dividends, loans, interest, patent royalties and licensing fees by the affiliation privilege under the Dutch tax legislation, grants significant tax planning opportunities to foreign companies.

Attraction of Holland

The location of Holland in Europe as a convenient place to set up a trading center, management center, coordinating center for international operations combined with the special advantages granted to foreign source income gives Holland a very special advantage.

Use of the treaty network

If the Dutch holding company is in turn a subsidiary of a company resident in a country which has concluded a double taxation treaty with the Netherlands, the withholding tax on the distribution of dividends is often reduced to as little as 5% or may even be reduced to zero. This is generally the case if there is a 25% minimum holding of the equity share capital. Thus, when the country of the parent company's residence provides for a dividend income deduction, (for example Belgium or

7. Parliament Document 6000 session 1962-63 page 25 and see also 13 European Taxation 433 December 1973.

France) and Middle East income is tax free, no corporate tax is levied at any stage.

The withholding tax rates applicable to dividends in relation to payments by a Dutch company to a parent company in other important investing jurisdictions can be summarised as follows:

Country of Residence of the company receiving the dividend	Under the Double taxation treaties receiving company holds 25% participation	Under the double taxation treaties receiving company holds less than 25% participation
Belgium	5	15
France	5	15
Germany	10	25
Japan	10	15
United Kingdom	5	15
United States	5	15

3. *Advance rulings*

In case of doubt on the application of the participation exemption to a particular case an advance ruling may be obtained of the Dutch tax administration's view from the Inspector dealing with the Company concerned; until recently these rulings could be obtained from the Ministry of Finance in cases where no Inspector had been appointed (including the case where a proposed company had not been formed). If the activity of the holding company is combined with financing or headquarter operations it is normally possible to obtain an advance ruling from the Inspector as to what will be subject to corporate tax in Holland. In normal cases a company engaged in financing operations can expect to be subject to 8% corporate tax on what is deemed Dutch source income. In the case of headquarter operations a percentage (usually 15%) of certain specified operational expenses will be deemed to be the taxable profit.

H. Comparability of Tax

Problems may arise with the Dutch tax authorities as they may decide that the Middle East tax on income is not comparable to the Dutch corporate tax. This position could be taken in Saudi Arabia and possibly other Gulf States. As a result all benefits resulting from the affiliation privilege and the unilateral relief measures would be lost.

The authorities could arrive to this conclusion on the basis of a 'side remark' made by the court during a hearing.[8] This remark was never contested later on during the case nor has it been reviewed by the tax authorities.

After having analysed the Saudi Tax on Income and the tax decrees in the Gulf States a strong case can be made out that the Saudi or Gulf Income tax is effectively a tax on corporate profits and therefore the Saudi Income should be subject to tax exemption in the Netherlands.

The position of any Dutch investor or any investor using Holland can be summarised broadly by stating that Advance rulings are likely to be available accepting tax comparability particularly if the consequences of denying it will be to cause the company to be formed outside the Netherlands.

I. Foreign Interest or Patent Royalties

Unless they are received through a permanent establishment subject to tax abroad, patent royalties and interest received from abroad are subject to corporate tax without credit for foreign taxes paid, but after deduction of foreign tax.

There are special regulations for interest and royalties received from developing countries.[9] These regulations are different to the usual regulations for the avoidance of double taxation. They enable a Dutch resident taxpayer to credit the foreign tax withheld or reduce its tax payable proportionately (whichever is the lower), provided that these royalties or interests are taxed in the country of origin and do not form part of the taxpayer's foreign gross income.

J. Withholding Tax

There is a withholding tax of 25% on dividend distribution for which credit is available against personal income tax.

No tax is withheld if the dividend is paid to a resident company which has a qualifying holding (under the affiliation privilege).

There is no withholding tax on interest.

There is no withholding tax on royalties.

8. Decision of Hoge Raad April 3, 1974, No. 17.259, BNB 1974/172, see also Weekblad voor fiscaal recht No. 5203 of November 21, 1974; the case was to decide whether or not a permanent establishment of the Dutch company existed in Saudi Arabia and therefore as a result whether or not the unilateral relief measures could be of application. In the course of the judgment an incidental observation stated that anyway the relief measures did not apply since Saudi Arabia income tax was not a tax on profits similar to Dutch corporation income tax.

9. Article 3a Unilateral Decree for the Avoidance of Double Taxation.

Chapter VI
United Kingdom

Corporation Income Tax

A. Basic Principles

A company which is resident in the UK is liable to corporation tax on the whole of its profits, namely income and chargeable (i.e. capital) gains, wherever these arise.

A company is resident for UK tax purposes in the country in which the central management and control of the conduct and policy of its business is exercised.[1] Although a company registered in the UK will not be regarded as a UK resident company, if it is centrally managed and controlled abroad, the Inland Revenue are likely to presume that UK registered companies are UK resident unless the contrary can be clearly proved.

B. Tax Rates

Corporation tax is fixed annually in arrear for financial years, which run from 1st April to 31st March and are denominated according to the year in which they commence. The rate of corporation tax for the financial year 1976 is 52%.

However, since for corporation tax the chargeable gains are reduced by a specified fraction (11/26 for the year to March 31st, 1977), the effective rate on chargeable gains is 30%.

A company resident in the UK is liable to account to the Inland Revenue for Advance Corporation Tax (ACT) in respect of qualifying distributions which include dividends. For the financial year 1976/77 the rate of ACT is 35/65th of the actual dividend paid. Any ACT paid by a company is available to reduce its liability for corporation tax on income, subject to fulfilling certain conditions. The mainstream corporation tax is therefore the corporation tax remaining payable after set-off for ACT.

It should be noted that:

a) ACT may not be deducted from corporation tax payable on chargeable capital gains or on development gains;

1. Section 246 Income and Corporation Tax Act 1970 (ICTA 1970).

b) ACT set-off is limited to that amount of ACT which would have been payable in respect of a distribution made at the end of that period of an amount which together with the ACT so payable in respect of it, is equal to the company's income charged to corporation tax for that period.

C. Double Taxation Relief Provisions

As seen, companies resident in the United Kingdom are taxed on their worldwide income and chargeable gains.

Double taxation relief is provided either by agreement with other countries[2], or, if there is no such agreement, unilateral relief can be claimed.[3] In both cases, relief is given by reducing UK taxes by the amount of credit due. The method of giving relief described hereafter applies to both cases.

The relief provided[4] consists of a tax credit, of the foreign tax suffered by the UK resident company, against UK corporation tax payable on the same income or gains.

The amount of credit for foreign tax to be allowed against corporation tax is restricted to a maximum of the corporation tax attributable to that income.[5] Any excess not credited is totally lost and is not even deductible as an expense. Bad tax planning could result in a loss of foreign tax credit. This would be the case in a company which by taking advantage of investment relief[6] would not be able to use all the foreign tax credit available. In such cases, the postponement of capital allowances should be envisaged in order to secure double taxation relief.

Relief may be given for those foreign taxes which correspond to UK corporate tax on income or tax on chargeable gains. A list of admissible and inadmissible taxes has been published by the Inland Revenue, but as a general rule, foreign taxes on profits are deductible, whereas foreign taxes based on turnover are not usually deductible.

Where no relief for foreign tax is available or if an election[7] is made by the taxpayer that credit shall not be used, the taxable foreign income for UK taxation purposes is the amount of foreign income less the foreign tax paid.

2. Section 497 ICTA 1970.
3. Section 498 ICTA 1970.
4. Section 501 ICTA 1970.
5. Section 505 ICTA 1970.
6. DSee page 135.
7. Section 515 ICTA 1970.

As seen before a company pays advance corporation tax in respect of dividends. The ACT paid is then used to reduce the company's liability for corporation tax on income, but this is in priority to any foreign tax credit which would otherwise be due against the same income. As a result a company paying dividends in excess of its UK income in a particular year may lose part of the potential foreign tax credit on its overseas income.

Therefore in some years, it may be necessary to restrict dividends in order to maximise any double tax relief. When foreign tax exceeds mainstream corporation tax, the unrelieved foreign tax cannot be carried forward or back and is therefore lost. An election may be made not to claim double tax relief[8] in which case foreign tax paid is deductible as an expense in computing profits chargeable to corporation tax.

It may also be advantageous to put overseas investments into a separate UK resident company in the group (preferably a subsidiary) and one which has no expenditure to set against its overseas investment income. This can then enable double tax relief to be claimed by that company without it affecting dividend policy by use either of the provisions for surrender of ACT or, more probably the facility for paying intra-group dividends without ACT.

D. Branches Abroad

a) Statute Law

A UK resident company with branches overseas is subject to corporation tax[9] on profits of those branches, irrespective of whether those profits have been remitted to the UK. Relief can be claimed in respect of unremittable overseas income whereby the tax charge may be postponed by agreement with the Inland Revenue.[10] If the income has been subject to foreign tax and such income is subject to UK tax also, double tax relief (or alternatively unilateral relief where no double tax treaties are in force) is available by way of a credit against the UK corporation tax liability attributable to that income.

In the case of losses of the overseas branch, such losses may be set off against UK profits.

b) Basis of Charge

All profits and losses from a branch are consolidated, whether the branch is situated in the UK or overseas. All expenditure incurred wholly

8. Section 511 ICTA 1970.
9. Section 243 ICTA 1970.
10. Section 418 ICTA 1970.

and exclusively for the purposes of the trade are deductible for tax purposes and in addition allowances for capital expenditure may be claimed. A lengthy list of items which are not deductible from profits has been provided.

Any loan between the parent company and its branch would contradict the principle of a single taxable entity. As a result all financial transactions should be passed through a current account. No interest should be charged on this account, although it would be feasible to apportion any head office charges to the branch (this charge to be treated as an expense in computing the branch profits).

Indirect methods of profit computation (profit being a percentage of turnover) are not generally acceptable for tax purposes.

c) Treaty Situation

The profits of the foreign branch are taxable in the foreign country and in general, the United Kingdom renounces in the Double Taxation Agreement, the sole right to tax the foreign branch. In the foreign country, the branch is considered as a separate entity of the company as a whole and the profits realised by it are those which it would realise if it was acting as a separate enterprise engaged in the same activity. The computation of branch profits for foreign tax purposes will thus depend on local law and not on United Kingdom rules. At the same time, from the UK point of view, it must be stressed that foreign branch and UK head office are the same entity although treaties usually provide for branch profits to be computed, as if they were separate enterprises dealing at arm's length.

Normally no profits are attributed to the branch where it purchases goods for the parent company.

E. Participation in Foreign Entities

A UK company may participate in foreign entities by holding an equity interest in those entities, and would be subject to UK corporation tax on income which it receives from such an entity by way of dividends.

When the UK company receives dividends from the non-resident company in which it has an equity participation, relief is available for overseas tax directly charged on the dividend, such as dividend withholding tax.

However, where the UK company holds, directly or indirectly[11] at least 10% of the voting power of the foreign company, relief by way of credit is available on any underlying overseas tax on profits actually paid up to a

11. Section 498 (4) ICTA 1970 or by treaty.

maximum of the UK corporation tax payable on the same profits. Thus relief applies to the direct tax charged on the dividend, but also to the foreign corporate tax on the profits out of which the dividend is paid. This credit for underlying tax may cover profits tax not only of the country of which that company is a resident, but also tax in any other territory, even the UK, where the profits out of which the dividend has been paid have suffered tax in that territory. The tax credit also takes into account any tax payable by a third company distributing dividends to the non-resident subsidiary of the UK company which in turn distributes dividends to the UK company, to the extent that relief would be given for the tax if the dividend had been paid by a non-resident company to a UK company, and similarly for companies further removed along a chain of qualifying shareholdings.

Thus, a United Kingdom parent company receiving dividends from a non-resident affiliate will in practice be entitled to the indirect credit for taxes paid by a whole chain of companies which are attributable to the ultimate dividend as far as each company owns a qualifying shareholding of at least 10% of the voting power in the company being the next link in the chain.[12]

In computing the UK tax on foreign income and the foreign tax credit, the net foreign income received is grossed up at the rate of foreign tax. The gross foreign income is then included in the taxable base and the foreign tax is credited, insofar as it does not exceed the UK tax on the gross foreign income.[13]

Here again the tax credit relief available may be restricted because the ACT payable as a result of dividend distributions represents the minimum corporation tax payable on the profits.

Loans and other transactions with subsidiaries: The UK anti-avoidance legislation[14] applies to transactions between UK and non-UK associated companies. Broadly this legislation enables UK Inland Revenue to substitute arm's length prices to counteract any loss of UK taxable revenue. As a result a UK company may be treated as if it had received or paid arm's length rates of interest or arm's length prices for the sale of goods or services.

F. Notional Tax

Double taxation agreements negotiated by the UK may treat as tax paid any foreign tax that would have been paid but for sparing arrangements.

12. Sections 498(4) and 508 ICTA 1970 or by relevant treaty.
13. Section 503 ICTA 1970.
14. Section 485 (3) ICTA 1970.

This means that any tax which would have been payable in a foreign country, but for a relief under the law of that territory given with a view to providing industrial, commercial, scientific, educational or other development therein can nevertheless be treated for purposes of credit against UK taxes as if it had been paid.[15]

This provision is of potential importance to United Kingdom companies with operations in Sudan (once the treaty between the Sudan and the United Kingdom has been ratified) as this country grants material tax exemptions (by way of investment incentive) to approved manufacturing activities in its territory.

G. Group Relief

'Where a UK resident company holds directly or indirectly, at least 75% of the issued ordinary share capital of one or more UK resident subsidiary companies, and is entitled to 75% of profits available for distribution and assets in a winding up, losses of one company in the group can be set off against the profits of another company within the same group for the corresponding accounting period.' It should be noted that it is only the trading losses, management expenses and excess charges on income which may be so relieved. Capital losses, for example, may not be surrendered.

H. Foreign Interest or Patent Royalties

When a UK resident company receives patent royalties and interest from abroad, the following rules apply: The foreign interest or patent royalties income is included in the taxable base of the company. If a foreign tax was levied on the interest or patent royalties, the income must be grossed up at the appropriate rate of foreign tax. A credit is available for the amount of UK tax payable on the grossed up income. In a treaty situation interest and patent royalties are often exempt from tax in the country of origin. In these cases there will be no direct credit in the UK and UK taxes will be charged in full.

I. Withholding Taxes

Double tax relief would normally be available for any withholding tax on dividends, interest, royalties or fee income receivable from outside the UK which are subject to UK income or corporation tax in the terms of the

15. Section 997 (3) ICTA 1970.

appropriate double taxation treaty or under the provisions of unilateral relief.

J. Investment Relief and Stock Relief

Accounting depreciation and amortisation of capital expenditure is not an allowable deduction in computing the profits subject to tax. However, relief is given by way of allowances, currently at 100% of cost for many assets although lower rates apply in certain instances. There is an option to claim less than 100% first year allowances on capital expenditure.[16] A recapture of allowances may follow subsequent sale of the assets.

Since 1974 relief has been given for the increase in inventory values of a company over an accounting period and currently the relief is allowed as a trading expense. Any decrease in the value of stock or the removal of the company from the ambit of UK Corporation tax, would result in a recapture of the relief, which would be treated as a trading receipt.

K. Anti Avoidance Measures[17]

Treasury consent is required for all the following transactions:

— Removal abroad of residence of a body corporate previously resident in the UK,
— Transfer to a non-resident of the trade or any part thereof, of a resident body corporate,
— In the case of resident body corporate causing or allowing a non-resident body corporate which it controls to create or issue shares or debentures,
— Transfer by a resident body corporate to any person of shares or debentures owned by it in a non-resident body corporate which it controls.

The Treasury is able to exercise a close supervision on the use of tax havens by United Kingdom companies and in most cases insists on 66% of the available foreign profits being remitted to the United Kingdom.

16. Section 41 (3) Finance Act 1971. This is an addition to the provisions of Section 515 ICTA 1970 mentioned on page 130.
17. Section 482 ICTA 1970.

Chapter VII
United States

Corporation Income Tax

A. Basic Principles

Companies incorporated in the US are taxable on their global income (worldwide income).

There are a number of corporations to which special taxation rules are applied. These include DISC's (Domestic International Sales Corporation)[1], Foreign Personal Holding Companies[2], tax-option corporations, real estate investment trusts, Western Hemisphere trade corporations, banks, insurance companies and cooperatives.

It should be noted that partnership income is assessed to tax on individual partners, whether persons or companies, whether the income is distributed or not.

B. Tax Rates

Taxable profits are chargeable to corporate tax at the following rates:
20% on the first $ 25,000 of taxable income,
22% on all income exceeding $ 25,000,
26% surtax on all income exceeding $ 50,000.

Undistributed 'personal holding company income' of a defined personal holding company is subject to tax of 70%.

Accumulated Earnings Tax: In addition to liability for the regular income taxes, every corporation other than a domestic or foreign personal holding company, a DISC, or an exempt organisation is liable for an extra tax (in the nature of a penalty) if it is formed or availed of for the purpose of evading the imposition of the income tax upon its shareholders, or the

1. See page 138.
2. See page 140.

shareholders of any other corporation, through the medium of permitting earnings or profits to accumulate instead of being divided or distributed.[3]

The rates of tax on disallowed accumulations, applicable to all corporations subject to this tax are:

$27\frac{1}{2}\%$ on the first $ 100,000 of the 'accumulated taxable income' and
$38\frac{1}{2}\%$ on the remainder of 'accumulated taxable income'.

In order to justify an accumulation of income, there must be a reasonable business need for it and a definite plan for its use. Since a corporation is given a credit for its reasonable business needs (including reasonably anticipated needs) in computing the accumulated earnings tax, the resolution of most disputes hinges on this issue.

C. Double Taxation Relief Provisions

A foreign tax credit may be elected (rather than taking a deduction) for foreign income taxes paid or accrued related to foreign source income. Credit may also be claimed for the underlying foreign income taxes paid or accrued on dividends received by a domestic corporation from its foreign subsidiaries through the third tier. (Each foreign subsidiary must own 10% of the next, and the overall indirect interest of the domestic corporation must be at least 5%.)

The credit was formerly calculated under either a per-country or an overall limitation. However, the tax reform act of 1976[4] repealed the per-country foreign tax credit limitation for all taxpayers. Under the per-country foreign tax credit limitation, taxes from a given country are applied only to income sourced in that country. This method was advantageous for the taxpayer when losses arising in one foreign country might otherwise reduce the allowable foreign tax credit related to other countries. In the future income and related taxes from all foreign sources are combined in computing the foreign tax credit. This method is advantageous when some foreign taxes are higher and other lower than the US rate of 48%. Withholding taxes normally qualify as income taxes.

Closely connected with the repeal of this per country limitation, is a new provision which will require all taxpayers to 'recapture' foreign losses[5] previously used to offset US taxable income. Previously, foreign losses did not affect a subsequent years' credit. The new recapture mechanism may result in an adjustment of the allowable foreign tax credits in a subsequently profitable year, since under this mechanism, a portion of subsequent foreign source income is recharacterized as US source income.

When a domestic corporation receiving a dividend from a 10% or more

3. Sections 531-537 Income Revenue Code.
4. Section 1031, 1976 Tax Reform Act.
5. Section 1032, 1976 Tax Reform Act.

owned foreign company elects to take credit for the foreign income tax levied upon the foreign subsidiary's accumulated profits that are the basis of the dividend, the domestic company must include in income not only the dividend but the foreign tax paid by the subsidiary. This also applies when taking the credit for the underlying foreign income taxes of second and third tier foreign corporations.

In situations where a US shareholder of a controlled foreign corporation is required to include undistributed earnings in income[6], the foreign tax credit is available.

Unused foreign taxes may be carried back two years and forward five years.

D. Domestic International Sales Corporation (DISC)

The Revenue Act of 1971 made it possible for corporations engaged in exports to obtain substantial tax savings by using a special type of company called a Domestic International Sales Corporation.

Definition[7]

DISC is a company incorporated in the US which issues only one class of stock, has a paid up capital of $ 2,500 and chooses to be treated as a DISC.

The basis requirements are that at least 95% of gross receipts and assets be qualified (i.e. export related):

Exports are considered as such if they are sold to be used abroad and are not ultimately used in the States.

The following qualify as export related:

Merchandise to be exported, assets used for export operations, receivables resulting from export operations, loans to export producers and shares of some related foreign international sales corporation, or of some unrelated foreign companies if the share acquisition will assist exports but is not more than 10% of the voting power of the foreign company.

At the end of the fiscal year a DISC must own qualified export assets which on the adjusted fiscal bases comprise at least 95% of the total adjusted assets.

In determining the taxable income of a DISC, the usual inter-company pricing rules of Section 482 can be relaxed. Thus, for example, sales by a manufacturing parent to its DISC export subsidiary need not be at arm's length, if the price charged is within specified 'safe harbors'. Similar rules apply to rentals.

6. See Controlled Foreign Corporation page 140 and Foreign Personal Holding Company page 140.
7. IRC See 992 a.

Tax Treatment

The 1976 tax reform curtailed the DISC provisions by the adoption of the so-called incremental approach to the computation of the DISC's deemed distribution. Congress concluded that the DISC provisions were not increasing export sales as originally intended and that this incremental approach would help expand export operations. To understand the new computations, it is useful to consider:

The old provisions: Basically a DISC is not liable to corporate tax. 50% of a DISC's taxable income was taxable in the hands of the shareholders even if no distribution had taken place. Tax on the other 50% could be deferred until the income was actually distributed or until the company ceased to be a DISC. 50% of the income could thus be deferred indefinitely and be used for other export operations.

New Provisions:[8] The current provisions provide that companies may take their tax benefits only on export sales that exceed 67% of those they made during the base period. To calculate the increase in export income of the year, a four-year base period is used. Through 1979 the base period is 1972 to 1975. After 1979, the earliest year will be dropped and the following year (1976...) will be added. For example, for the year 1980 the base period is 1973 to 1976.

Example

	Old Law	*New Law*
1. DISC taxable income (on sales of $ 740,000)	$ 200,000	$ 200,000
Total Export Gross Receipts in base period = $ 2,000,000 divided by (- 4) = $ 5,00,000 'Adjusted base period export gross receipts' (67%) $ 335,000		
2. Taxable income attributed to base period		(90,000)[9]
3. DISC adjusted taxable income		110,000
4. 'Deemed Distribution' 50%	(100,000)	(55,000)
5. Accumulated DISC income	100,000	55,000
6. Total deemed distribution for 1976 (Lines 2 + 4)	$ 100,000	$ 145,000

8. Section 1101, 1976 Tax Reform Act.

9. $\frac{335,000}{740,000}$ = 45% x $ 200,000 = (90,000).

E. Branches Abroad

Income from overseas branches is fully included in the US corporation's taxable income.

Losses of overseas branches may be set off against US profits. But as explained before, in the future, an overall foreign loss in one year may affect subsequent year's credit. However, net operating losses may first be carried back for three years and then forward for seven years until absorded.

As discussed above, a foreign tax credit may reduce the US tax on foreign source earnings.

F. Participations in Foreign Entities

When anything more than negligible US ownership of foreign corporate shares exists, complex US tax laws are applied.

A Controlled Foreign Corporation[10] is defined as a foreign corporation in which on any day of the taxable year more than 50% of the voting interest is owned by US corporations, partnerships or individuals, each of whom owns directly or constructively 10% or more of the voting interest. If such control exists, the US shareholders owning at least 10% may be taxed on part of the corporation's undistributed income. US shareholders must include in their gross income certain types of foreign income (called subpart F Income) of a passive nature and foreign base company sales and services income.

A Foreign Personal Holding Company[11] is defined as a foreign company in which more than 50% in value of the outstanding stock is owned directly or indirectly by five or fewer US citizens or residents and at least 60% (50% after the first taxable year) of the gross income consists of dividends, interest, royalties, annuities, rents (unless amounting to 50% or more of gross income), gains in security transactions, income from personal service contracts and certain other types of income. When these conditions are fulfilled, the US shareholder is subject to tax on the undistributed as well as the distributed income of the foreign company as though the income had been distributed in the form of dividends.

In most other situations involving US corporations' holdings in foreign companies, the dividends are included in income and a foreign tax credit is permitted to reduce the US tax on such earnings.

Internal Revenue Code Section 482 must always be considered where any two or more companies, businesses, etc., are owned or controlled directly or indirectly by the same interests. This section covers inter-

10. Sections 951, 957, 958 IRC.
11. Sections 551-558 IRC.

company pricing and any other allocations of income, deductions, credits, etc., between related companies. The Internal Revenue Service may reapportion such pricing or allocations where it considers that taxes are being evaded or income is not being clearly reflected.

Where one member of a group of related entities makes a loan or an advance directly or indirectly to another member of the group, the regulations require that an arm's length interest charge be made. An 'arm's length interest rate' is defined as the rate of interest which was charged, or would have been charged at the time the indebtedness arose, in independent transactions with or between unrelated parties under similar circumstances. The regulations state that among the factors to be considered are the amount and duration of the loan, the security involved, the credit standing of the borrower, and the interest rate prevailing at the situs of the lender or creditor for comparable loans.

G. Foreign Bribes and International Boycotts

The 1976 tax reform[12] introduces regulations for foreign 'bribes' and international boycotts.

With respect to foreign 'bribes', the Act provides that any payments regarded as being 'bribes', as defined[13] will be treated as a deemed dividend to the US shareholders of the corporations (foreign subsidiaries or Domestic International Sales Corporations) making such payments. In addition, the entity making the payment will not be allowed to reduce its earnings and profits by the amount of the payments.

The international boycott provision denies certain tax benefits (deferral of tax on foreign earnings, deferral of tax on DISC earnings and foreign tax credit) on a limited basis, to those taxpayers participating in or cooperating with an international boycott. Extensive definitional ground rules are provided in order to determine when a taxpayer participates in or cooperates with an international boycott. In addition, a formula is set forth for use in determining what portion, if any, of a taxpayers' tax benefits will be forfeited by cooperating with or participating in this type of activity. In lieu of using this formula a taxpayer may specifically identify the income and foreign taxes attributable to foreign operations in order to determine the amount of tax benefits denied.

Finally, special reports will be required to be filed with the Secretary of the Treasury to help determine when and to what extent the prohibited activity is taking place.

In determining whether particular transactions will lead to denial of foreign tax credit, it is necessary to consider the following key questions:

12. Section 1061-1067, 1976 Tax Reform Act.
13. Section 162 (c) of the code.

— Does a specific activity or transaction constitute cooperation with or participation in a boycott?
— If so, is such activity sufficient to create a presumption that all transactions with the country are boycott related?

H. Affiliation Privilege

Corporations which receive dividends from members of an 'affiliated group' and which do not file consolidated income tax returns are allowed a 100% deduction for qualifying dividends from members. There are various technical concessions that are made in exchange for this 100% deduction. This does not generally apply to dividends paid by foreign corporations.

Corporations which are either ineligible for the 100% dividend deduction or which do not elect it, are entitled to a special deduction from gross income for dividends received from a domestic corporation itself subject to tax. The deduction amounts to 85% of the dividends received, but generally not exceeding 85% of the taxable income of the recipient, computed without regard to the net operating loss deduction and dividends received deduction. The 85% deduction for dividends received applies to dividends from a foreign corporation which has been engaged in a trade or business in the US for an uninterrupted period of at least 36 months, or less if the corporation has not been in existence for that period, and at least 50% of whose gross income is effectively connected with its US business. The deduction is allowed only for 85% of the dividends attributable to income effectively connected with a US trade or business.

I. Withholding Tax

The US withholding tax applies only to income from US sources. Payment from an entity located in the US does not in itself constitute US source income. If a US company has only fee income, earned for services rendered entirely outside the US, a dividend paid by such company would not be subject to the withholding tax. Interest and dividend income paid by a US company whose gross income is composed of at least 80% foreign source income (and has been for three years) is considered to be fully foreign source and not subject to US withholding.

Index

GPSR Compliance

The European Union's (EU) General Product Safety Regulation (GPSR) is a set of rules that requires consumer products to be safe and our obligations to ensure this.

If you have any concerns about our products, you can contact us on ProductSafety@springernature.com

In case Publisher is established outside the EU, the EU authorized representative is:

Springer Nature Customer Service Center GmbH
Europaplatz 3
69115 Heidelberg, Germany

Batch number: 10844827

Printed by Printforce, the Netherlands